# FLYER'D UP!

# BRIAN STARTARE

## FOREWORD BY:
## JIM JACKSON

Trivia, Facts, and Anecdotes for
Fans of the Orange and Black.

Brian Startare is a local radio sportscaster in Philadelphia. He currently is the pre, inter-mission and post game host for Philadelphia Flyers hockey in addition to hosting his own radio show on nights and weekends on Sportsradio 610-WIP.

FLYER'D UP! Trivia, Facts and Anecdotes for Fans of the Orange and Black
Copyright © 2009 Brian Startare
All Rights Reserved
First Published 2009
Printed in the United States of America

ISBN: 978-0-578-00861-5

Digital Composition: Sean Miller
Proofreader: Meredith Bajgier
Illustrator: Chris Tucci

Photo Credits: Len Redkoles, Bruce Bennett, and Ed Mahan

This book is published with permission granted by The Philadelphia Flyers and The National Hockey League.

Publisher
Sports Challenge Network
Philadelphia, PA 19102
www.sportschallengenetwork.com
email: sales@sportschallengenetwork.com

# DEDICATION -

*To Andrea and Chase-My Family...My Love Always*
*To My Family-Mom, Denise, Lisa, Peter...Thank you for being there*
*To Dad...you are missed*
*And*
*To All Flyer Fans...Orange and Black Forever*

# TABLE OF CONTENTS

# TABLE OF CONTENTS

# FOREWORD BY
# Jim Jackson

If there is one constant that has stood the test of time through my 16 years as a broadcaster of the Philadelphia Flyers, it has been the passion of the multitudes of fans of the Orange and Black. Through the good times and the bad (and there really haven't been too many of those), Flyers' fans are there with unbridled enthusiasm, a desire for excellence, and a thirst for anything that is in the smallest way having to do with their hometown hockey team.

It is fitting then that within these pages, these fans are given a very healthy dose of all that is the Flyers and their remarkable history from one of their own. Brian Startare exemplifies the energy and dedication that is behind the passion of a true Philadelphia Flyers fan. His development into such an ardent supporter of this franchise is probably not unlike that of many of the same people who will read this book. The only difference is that Brian has had the incredible fortune to be able to grow up and then cover the team he so loved as a youngster.

But Brian's position as a talk show host and reporter serves Flyers' fans well in Flyer'd Up! It allowed him access to so many of the Flyer players to help make this book enjoyable for the people who love to revel in the tremendous tradition of the Philadelphia franchise. From Angotti to Richards, and Parent to Biron, and from Allen to Stevens, there is something for everyone.

It is presented in a unique format with lists, quizzes, and narrative. It will settle some arguments and ignite some others, but for any Flyers fan, Flyer'd Up! is a great way to relive some of the great moments and reacquaint one with some of the great players in team history.

Enjoy Flyer fans! Flyer'd Up! is here to help satisfy your insatiable hunger for Flyers' fodder. Let your incredible passion for Flyers hockey live on........

# ACKNOWLEDGMENTS

There are many people who helped along the way in the completion of this project.

I would like to thank the NHL for granting its permission for this project and to the entire Philadelphia Flyers organization. Special thanks to Senior Vice president of Business Operations Shawn Tilger, Chairman Ed Snider, President and COO Peter Luukko, Vice president of Public Relations Ike Richman, Senior Director of Communications Zach Hill and the rest of their wonderful staffs. A special thanks to Joe Klueg, Joe Kadlec, Kevin Kurz, Lindsey Domers, Shauna Adams, Sharon Allison, Linda Mantai, Lauren Cochran, Missy Keeler, Jill Lipson, Lou Nolan, Lauren Hart, Brian McBride and Betsy Brubaker-McGill. And of course to all of the many players who have worn the orange and the black, especially those who participated in the interview process of this project.

Thank you to my colleagues at Sportsradio 610WIP for their support, most notably to Angelo Cataldi, for giving me an opportunity and for setting the example on how things are done the correct way. Thank you Rhea Hughes, Glen Macnow, and Big Daddy Graham for your support, friendship and advice. Thank you to the entire on-air staff, the outstanding sales and promotions department, especially Marc Farzetta for his continued assistance. To the producers, engineers and management, including General Manager Marc Rayfield and program directors Tom Lee and Andy Bloom for giving me the opportunity to do what I love as a career. A special thank you to Jason Myrtetus and Jill Speckman in the programming department for their continued support. And of course to all of our fantastic listeners and callers. What a great place to work.

Thank you to Eli Kowalski for his countless hours of hard work and advice. To Chris Tucci for his brilliant illustrations.

Thank you to the wonderful folks at CN8 television including Seth Maga-lener, Greg Murphy, Jeff Shurrila, Tim Walton, Geoff Camlin, Torie McCo-nnell, Debbie Foster and the entire television crew.

To the Philadelphia Flyers broadcasters and beat writers for showing me the ropes; Jim Jackson, Keith Jones, Bill Clement, Tim Saunders, Chris Therien, Brian Propp, Sam Carchidi, Ed Moran, Tim Pinacchio and Chuck Gormley. A special thank you to Bill Meltzer, and Anthony San Filippo for their outstanding ideas and contributions to this project for which I am forever grateful.

And thank you once again to Glen Macnow and Al Morganti for their con-tributions and assistance.

To all the wonderful and loyal fans of the Flyers for their help with this proj-ect, including Bob and Shawn Hill, Jo Anne Burke and Todd Flynn. And a special thank you to the late Greg Ficchi, for there is not a bigger Flyers fan in heaven.

And most of all, and most importantly to all of my family and friends for their support. To my wife Andrea and our son Chase, for allowing me to work in an industry that doesn't always lend itself to family time. My mother Ruth for her unwavering love and support. My Father Pete who is watching over me from above. My brother Pete for being my best friend and my sisters Denise and Lisa for their support and love. Thank you also to my wonder-ful in-laws whose support and help is appreciated greatly. And lastly thanks to the entire Nob Hill Hockey Crew, Eric, Jimmy, Keith, Tommy, Danny, Norm, and Pete, for that's where the love of the great game of hockey and for the Philadelphia Flyers began.

If I forgot anyone else, thank you also!

# INTRODUCTION

My earliest, most vivid memory takes me back to the age of five. That year, I went to school for the first time to take placement tests for kindergarten. By the time I had finished, I shocked the school's administrators and teachers with my flawless recitation of the entire 1974-1975 Flyers roster. I had already known the Flyers well for the two years leading up to the tests and, for the rest of my life, they would continue to be a part of me. The Philadelphia hockey team was as much a part of my childhood as my own family, and to this day, the Flyers remain my brothers.

I played hockey on the streets in front of my parents' suburban home in South Jersey, which was only a few miles east of Philadelphia (and, too, the Flyers). My friends and I met outside nearly every day; we gave the worn-out asphalt only the summer months to rest from the constant pounding of our Kohos and Sherwoods. The instant we flew off the school bus, the game was on. The competitive battles only ended when our mothers' incessant shouting got to be too great and we were escorted inside to complete our homework. After I completed my work, I always turned back to hockey. If my friends and I weren't playing table rod hockey in the basement, we played floor hockey, using pizza boxes for waffle boards and crumpled up balls of aluminum foil for pucks.

I collected the all trading cards; I made miniature models of NHL buildings; I hung posters of the Canadiens' Frank Mahovolich and the Blue's

# FLYER'D UP!

Trivia, Facts, and Anecdotes for Fans of the Orange and Black.

Gary Unger on my bedroom walls. I adored Flyers hockey. The day was always more tolerable when there was a Flyers game to look forward to that evening. I, faithfully sitting in front of the TV night after night, didn't miss a game.

I lived, breathed and slept hockey. I knew the roster of every team, from the Cleveland Barons to the Chicago Blackhawks. Of course, I knew best the Flyers and loved them the most. I idolized Reggie Leach, Bobby Clarke, Bill Barber, and Bernie Parent; later, I followed Rick Tocchet, Peter Zezel and Mark Howe. I celebrated every victory like I had played on the line with Illka Sinisalo and took the losses to heart like I gave up the game-winner between the pipes alongside Ron Hextall. I thought Tom Bladon's shot was the hardest I'd ever seen and that Gordie Murphy's best trait was keeping the puck in at the blue line.

I first saw the Flyers live at the Spectrum on March 5, 1981. I still vividly remember their triumphant 10-1 win over the Winnipeg Jets and the glorified pride the win instilled in me. Dave Babych (who would later play for the Flyers towards the end of his career) played for the Jets that night. I yelled his name countless ties during warm-ups and pleaded for attention. Finally, he gave in to my constant stream of requests and handed me a puck. Since that day, I've attended hundreds of games. I hope to take my son, Chase, to hundreds more.

In the fall of 1986, I created a scrapbook that still sits in my attic. Alongside it are standard things kept in the long-lost corners of the home, like baseball cards and high school yearbooks. Every year, I take time to revisit the keep-

# FLYER'D UP!

Trivia, Facts, and Anecdotes for Fans of the Orange and Black.

sake that I created when I was just 15. It still amazes me how simple things must have been then - after all, I spent a lot of time to complete the project. I stay up in the attic each year a few more minutes than the last, recalling the times that I had with my Flyers family.

Inside the pages of my childhood are high gloss color pictures of Jimmy and Joe Watson, Bob Dailey and Dave Poulin. Photographs of a pimply-faced adolescent, posing alongside Brian Propp, Brad Marsh, Doug Crossman and the Stanley Cup adorn the pages of dank grey cardboard. A select few are autographed in fading black ink. Also contained in the book are various newspaper clippings, some from as far back as the 1975 Stanley Cup win over the Buffalo Sabres from The Evening Bulletin; others are from The Courier Post depicting the incredible playoff run of the 1984-1985 Flyers led by rookie coach Mike Keenan. Schedules and box scores decorate the pages, carefully juxtaposed with the creative mind of a teenager. All of the pages aren't filled with happy memories, though. The scrapbook includes the painful times, too. After all, this is Philadelphia.

My heart was broken by the Flyers on many occasions. After some agonizing losses, I was often reduced to tears. I went numb for days. That's the life of being a Philadelphia sports fan, I guess.

As losses came, none was bigger than the one on the morning of November 10, 1985. That day, I mourned the death of Flyers goaltender Pelle Lindbergh, who was killed in an automobile accident just 10 minutes from my home. He was one of my favorite players. I dealt with the reality of death for only the second time in my life. My grandfather died in 1980 and Lindbergh's passing produced the same broken heart.

# FLYER'D UP!

Trivia, Facts, and Anecdotes for Fans of the Orange and Black.

I must admit that for an instant I selfishly thought of the effect on the team. I knew that after Lindbergh's death, the Flyers had no chance of returning to glory that year. Not only did Philadelphia lose a great person, but also the game's best goaltender. Sure enough, the Rangers took the Flyers out in the first round of the playoffs. I still think of Lindbergh occasionally. In my scrapbook, I have a memorial to the loveable Swede, complete with his picture and autograph, along with a drawing of him I sketched after his death. I also have minute shards of glass and chips of red paint from his Porsche collected by my brother-in-law at the scene of the accident. I truly idolized Lindbergh.

My history with the Flyers begins with an early memory of Bob Kelly's stuffer in Game 6 of the 1975 Finals. Since then, vivid pictures have been etched deep in my mind that will never escape. I recall these shining times when I'm feeling low and, somehow, the immediate sensation of the specific game or play returns to me. I remember it all: Leach's 61 goals in 1975-76; a New Year's Eve loss in 1977 to the St. Louis Blues that left a 7 year-old in tears; Leon Stickle stealing my summer with a blown offside call in the 1980 Finals against the Islanders; Eric Lindros' historic arrival and embarrassing departure. I was there for the proud playoff wins and the devastating losses. The thousands of images include Orest Kinderchuk to Lindsay Carson, Ed Van Impe to Jeff Chychrun, Larry Goodenough to Jiri Latal. There's not a Flyer player since 1974 that I haven't at least uttered his name, watched him on the ice or read about him in a book. I have lived Flyers' history.

Now, 33 years after my kindergarten visit, fate has found me employed

by a radio station that is the sole rights holder of the team. Years ago, I aspired to be "The Voice" of the Flyers, Gene Hart. He was an idol in the broadcasting field; he helped me to learn the game and its nuances. Now, I reach to my history with fondness and take those lessons, experiences, and memories as fuel for my passion for the game of hockey. Every time I'm behind the microphone for a Flyers game, I take a short trip down memory lane. I still marvel at the fact that I'm the radio pre- and post-game host of the Philadelphia Flyers. My career defines the word fortunate. To a boy who knew everything about hockey and to a man who still does, being part of the game is a love I can't begin to describe.

At the age of 38, I have a lifetime of Flyers memories and so many stories to share. It's a blessing to have a career covering the sport I love and the team I adored so much as a boy. I hope that when reading this book, you enjoy the trivia, puzzles, pictures, lists and anecdotes. I have faith that you, the fan of the orange and black, will also experience the return of pleasant childhood memories and learn something new about the team along the way. Don't forget to have a fantastic time in the process, too!

CHRIS TULLI '05

Trivia, Facts, and Anecdotes for Fans of the Orange and Black.

# WHAT IT MEANS TO BE A FLYER

### *"I am, was and always will be a Philadelphia Flyer."*
### *--NHL and Flyers' Hall of Famer Bill Barber*

Growing up in the Delaware Valley, I had the pleasure of being a devout Flyers fan as a youth, enjoying the team's incredible successes. I also experienced (as an added bonus) a tremendous sense of satisfaction from so closely watching a team that was in many ways a family that invited you into its home on a nightly basis. They led by example and made you feel as though you were a part of the team. They were a hard-working crew that played for the logo on the front of their sweaters and not for the name on their backs. I still feel that way today; though now I am fortunate enough to be around the team on a regular basis and am able to watch them operate. In this way, I have gained even more respect for the club. Now, many years later, that simple flying P, with its four spreading wings, to me represents not only the team on the ice but also the ownership of the organization by the entire city of Philadelphia.

The Flyers' organization is indeed a rare breed; its bloodlines, first cast by creator Ed Snider in 1967, still flow not individually but broadly through the hearts of not only its players, employees and fans but also to a large and very close-knit community. The Flyers pump life and pride into the masses who revel in the great sport of hockey. They are a proud lineage passed through generations. If you ask those who have been fortunate enough to be touched by the Flyer family, they will claim that they are still connected to the organization with every fiber of their being. They will vow to maintain this bond for as long as they live. After all, they have no choice: once a Flyer, always a Flyer.

# FLYER'D UP!

Trivia, Facts, and Anecdotes for Fans of the Orange and Black.

It was my pleasure to sit down and talk with those who once donned the orange and black -- the representatives chosen to convey and personify the Flyer image. It was clear to me from my very first exchange that the meaning of "being a Flyer" included more than just what is seen on the sheet of ice, in the box scores or in the standings. Its exclusive membership carries a sense of intrinsic pride, respect and tradition that is carefully passed down as a priceless family heirloom. The times and players change, but the attitude lives on.

There are few organizations in professional sports that can consistently carry the core values that the Philadelphia Flyers maintain. In the ever-changing landscape of greed and mistrust in professional sports, it is rare to find players who have physically moved away from the organization that still feel as though they have emotionally never left. Still the Flyers are looked upon as not only a successful franchise, but also as leaders in their community. They are an example to other organizations. To the team, success is measured in winning not only on the ice, but off the ice as well. If you're wondering what I'm trying to explain, just read the following responses from players, and you'll know exactly what it means to be a Flyer.

### Lou Angotti (1967-68), Flyers' First Captain
"It was the best experience for me, the Flyers have never forgotten me and I have never forgotten them. They always have treated me well. I played on the very first team in Philadelphia and I even made it as a Trivial Pursuit question. I'll be a part of history forever as the first captain in team history."

### Gary Dornhoefer (1967-78)
"For me it was always a pride thing, I always coached on the idea to play for the crest on the front, not for your name on the back. It's the logo that counts. It represented the city and the team. When you work for one another

*Did you know that the Flyers were the first*
*expansion team ever to win the Stanley Cup?*

# FLYER'D UP!

Trivia, Facts, and Anecdotes for Fans of the Orange and Black.

and achieve a common goal, it's rewarding. All you have is your teammates on the ice, but in the end we were all in it together."

### Simon Nolet (1967-74)

"It meant more than I can express in words. Being there from the beginning, winning the Stanley Cup, that was the greatest. Being a Flyer is about winning."

### Keith Allen
### (former General Manager 1969-83)

"It means being a Champion. It means being highly competitive and in the fight every year. Players like to come to Philadelphia because they're treated very well and it's a winning tradition."

### Bob Clarke (1969-1984)

"I think the pride and commitment and being part of the winning tradition is what's it about. Being part of our team and our city, and what it meant to everyone involved, that feeling never goes way. The tradition that carries on that started in 1967 until today: once a Flyer, always a Flyer."

### Bob "Hound" Kelly (1970-80)

"It encompasses a lot of things. You have to start at the beginning, when an organization thinks so highly of you to let you wear their jersey, you are instantly instilled with pride and are poised to present a great work ethic. You're not only representing the Flyers, but the organization, the fans, and the entire city. It's all about the work ethic that keeps guys coming back to this place."

### Bill Clement (1971-1975)

"It was part of something legendary, something almost mystical. The lure

# FLYER'D UP!

Trivia, Facts, and Anecdotes for Fans of the Orange and Black.

of the Spectrum, the Kate Smith factor, the two Cups. It was being part of something that was going to be etched into the players involved and the millions of fans of the orange and black. It was more than just competing in a hockey uniform, it was an honor."

### Bobby "Chief" Taylor (1971-76)

"It's just having enormous pride in wearing that jersey. Our coach Fred Shero was big on the team concept, playing for one another. He pushed us to do that on and off the ice. Get out into the community, you just don't take, you give back. Being a Flyer is more than being a member of a sports team, it was giving back to an entire city and playing for the 20 guys in the dressing room and for everyone connected."

### Orest Kindrachuck (1972-1978)

"It's a tradition unlike any other, and it was built very early on when players respected the logo on the sweater, the hard work ethic. Once you were a Flyer it meant dedication and desire and, most of all, respect."

### Paul Holmgren (1975-1984)

"I came to Philadelphia as a player when I was 20 years old and got to play with all the great players of the winning teams. I got to play with Clarkie, Bill Barber, Bernie, Rick MacLeish, the Watson brothers, so I got an early idea of the culture of hard work and determination and grit and tenacity that it takes to be a part of the organization. Being a Flyer means that you're a blue collar guy and you get in there and put the hard work. It's a tremendous honor to play in the NHL and to be a Philadelphia Flyer."

### Brian Propp (1979-90)

"I was proud to represent the people of Philadelphia, to play for the emblem on the front of the jersey, and not my name on the back."

# FLYER'D UP!

Trivia, Facts, and Anecdotes for Fans of the Orange and Black.

### Tim Kerr (1980-1991)

"Simply, it means you are counted on to do your best at all times."

### Brad Marsh (1981-88)

"When I was traded there from Calgary, I thought wow, a Stanley Cup organization, I'm going to the best and toughest team in the NHL, and I was right. I was not disappointed. Coming to the Flyers changed my career for the better as I learned what it was all about."

### Illka Sinisalo (1981-90)

"Plain and simple, being a member of a great hockey family."

### Dave Brown (1982-89, 91-95)

"Being a Flyer was a huge sense of pride for me. They were the first NHL team to see something in me and I always have tried to return that loyalty."

### Mark Howe (1982-92)

"A tradition in place when the franchise began and the standards that were set by the Stanley Cup teams of the 70's. A sense of pride and honor lives within all of us who have earned the privilege to have worn the orange and black."

### Brad "The Beast" McCrimmon (1982-87)

"The Flyers tradition speaks for itself… always striving to reach the ultimate goals. It has always been that way. When you're a Flyer you try to reach the highest level with every effort."

### Ron Sutter (1982-91)

"Knowing that I played for that team for nine seasons and still 20 something years later, I still have that connection. It meant friendships, success and

*Did you know that only the Montreal Canadiens*
*have a better all-time winning percentage than the Flyers?*

# FLYER'D UP!

Trivia, Facts, and Anecdotes for Fans of the Orange and Black.

solid relationships with solid people. Once you're a Flyer, you always have that common bond. It still amazes me that every time I go back there, people still recognize me."

### Peter Zezel (1984-1988)
"It is the ultimate to be a Flyer, and you realize how important the Flyers are to the city of Philadelphia, and most importantly how great you are treated by the owner Ed Snider and the organization. Class."

### Scott Mellanby (1985-1991)
"Being a Flyer means a great deal of pride and character. The teams of the seventies established the type of team player a Flyer represents. I am very proud and thankful I got to start my career around people who personified these things."

### Craig "Chief" Berube (1986-91, 98-00)
"Being a Flyer is tradition, work ethic and giving it all you have. From Mr. Snider to Bobby Clark to Bernie Parent, it just keeps carrying on through the years. It boils down to the fans that demand hard work and success, that's what you play for."

### Ron Hextall (1986-1992, 94-99)
"I think it's hard to explain. You have to be inside to really know the feeling. The first time I ever put that jersey over my head for an exhibition game, I remember feeling such a great sense of pride, and that feeling has never left me."

### Keith Jones (1998-2001)
"It's almost like having an extended family. You marry into a family you like, a family without the mother in-law!"

# FLYER'D UP!

Trivia, Facts, and Anecdotes for Fans of the Orange and Black.

### Jeff Carter (2005-present)

"When you think of the Flyers, you think of the Broad Street Bullies and the tradition of the great players and great teams that come through here over the years and just to be a part of it, to try to go out and play hard every game and keep that tradition going. That's what it means to be a Flyer."

### Mike Richards (2005-present)

"It is nice to be a part of an organization that has so much tradition and it's always wanting to win. To play in the city that has tremendous pride for its hockey team and to represent this organization is all about pride."

### Marty Biron (2007-present)

"It's an enormous sense of pride to be a part of this organization. The passion from the fans, the incredible treatment from the organization. The history of the team runs deep. People here bleed the black and orange and it carries on through generations. When you see the pictures on the wall in the locker room and you see all the players that come back to his organization it's incredible. It's the team, the community, the fans. It's all a pride thing when you put on that jersey."

### Danny Briere (2007- present)

"It's pretty cool. The fans are excited about the hockey team and want us to win every night out. They care about their team. They push you to play harder and get better. No excuses. It's great to be part of an organization in which the hockey team itself means so much to the fans and I wouldn't change it for anything in the world."

# FLYER'D UP!

## 60's and 70's TRIVIA

1. Who was the first Flyer to score four goals in one game?
A. Gary Dornhoefer
B. Rick MacLeish
C. Bobby Clarke
D. Reggie Leach

2. The Flyers have had the first overall draft pick only once in their history. Who did they select with that pick?
A. Bill Barber
B. Brian Propp
C. Mel Bridgman
D. Behn Wilson

3. The first trade the Flyers made in franchise history was to send their first round pick in 1970 to the Boston Bruins (the Bruins selected Rick MacLeish with the pick). Who did the Flyers get in return?
A. Bernie Parent
B. Danny Schock
C. John McKenzie
D. Rosaire Paiement

4. Who was the first recipient of the Barry Ashbee Trophy, which recognizes the best Flyers defenseman in a season?
A. Joe Watson
B. Jimmy Watson
C. Bob Dailey
D. Andre Dupont

5. In 1976, the Flyers were the only NHL team to defeat the Soviet Red Army team during their tour of the league. Who was the only other team that didn't lose to the Soviets, instead playing to a 3-3 tie?
A. Boston Bruins
B. New York Rangers
C. Chicago Blackhawks
D. Montreal Canadiens

6. Who scored the fastest overtime playoff goal in Flyers history (23 seconds)?
A. Gary Dornhoefer
B. Andre Dupont
C. Bobby Clarke
D. Mel Bridgman

7. The Flyers drafted Bobby Clarke in the second round of the 1969 draft. Who did they draft in the first round that year?
A. Lew Morrison
B. Bob Currier
C. Bill Clement
D. Al Sarault

8. Who was the first goalie drafted by the Flyers to play in the NHL?
A. Jerome Mrazek
B. Reggie Lemelin
C. Michel Belhumeur
D. Rick St. Croix

26

**answers on page 179**

# FLYER'D UP!

Trivia, Facts, and Anecdotes for Fans of the Orange and Black.

## 60's and 70's TRIVIA

9. Who led the Flyers in goals in their inaugural season (1967-68)?
A. Leon Rochefort
B. Andre Lacroix
C. Lou Angotti
D. Gary Dornhoefer

10. Bobby Clarke led the Flyers in assists every season in the 1970s; one season he tied for the team lead. Who was he tied with?
A. Bill Barber
B. Reggie Leach
C. Rick MacLeish
D. Ken Linseman

11. What was the longest winning streak the successful Flyers put together in the '70s?
A. 9 games
B. 10 games
C. 11 games
D. 12 games

12. What team did the Flyers defeat 11-0 on Oct. 20, 1977 for the most lopsided shutout victory in franchise history?
A. Vancouver Canucks
B. Colorado Rockies
C. Pittsburgh Penguins
D. Atlanta Flames

13. The Flyers' regular season record for shots on goal in a game is 62 on April 1, 1976. What team did the Flyers face that night?
A. Pittsburgh Penguins
B. Washington Capitals
C. New York Rangers
D. New York Islanders

14. The Flyers have only played in two games in their history in which they were not penalized. The first was March 18, 1979. Who was the opponent?
A. Toronto Maple Leafs
B. St. Louis Blues
C. Detroit Red Wings
D. Chicago Black Hawks.

15. Who holds the team record for most shots on goal in one season with 380?
A. Reggie Leach
B. Bobby Clarke
C. Bill Barber
D. Rick MacLeish

16. What visiting player posted seven points in one game against the Flyers, the most allowed by Philadelphia in a regular season game?
A. Bobby Orr
B. Gilbert Perreault
C. Red Berenson
D. Guy LaFleur

27

**answers on page 179**

# FLYER'D UP!

Trivia, Facts, and Anecdotes for Fans of the Orange and Black.

## 60's and 70's TRIVIA

17. Who holds the Flyers' record for most penalty minutes in one game with 55?
A. Frank Bathe
B. Bob Kelly
C. Dave Schultz
D. Don Saleski

18. Who holds the Flyers' record for most playoff game-winning goals with 10?
A. Bill Barber
B. Reggie Leach
C. Bobby Clarke
D. Rick MacLeish

19. Mark Howe and Eric Desjardins, arguably the two best defensemen in Flyers history, rank numbers one and two on the team's list of playoff points scored by defensemen. Who is third?
A. Tom Bladon
B. Behn Wilson
C. Jimmy Watson
D. Bob Dailey

20. Who has played in more playoff games as a Flyer than any other defenseman?
A. Ed Van Impe
B. Joe Watson
C. Jimmy Watson
D. Andre Dupont

21. Who was the first Flyer to attempt a penalty shot?
A. Orest Kindrachuk
B. Bill Clement
C. Bill Barber
D. Rick MacLeish

22. Who was the first Flyer to score a goal on a penalty shot?
A. Orest Kindrachuk
B. Bill Clement
C. Bill Barber
D. Rick MacLeish

23. Who was the first opposing player to attempt and score a goal on a penalty shot against the Flyers?
A. Jocelyn Guevremont
B. Lanny McDonald
C. Richard Martin
D. Curt Bennett

24. The Flyers once traded their coach (Fred Shero) to the New York Rangers for a first round draft pick. Who did the Flyers select with that pick?
A. Brian Propp     B. Behn Wilson     C. Ken Linesman     D. Mel Bridgman

25. On May 15, 1973 the Flyers traded Doug Favell and a first round pick to Toronto for Bernie Parent and a second round pick. Who did the Flyers select with that second rounder?
A. Tom Bladon     B. Larry Goodenough     C. Jimmy Watson     D. Reggie Lemelin

28

**answers on page 179**

# FLYER'D UP!

Trivia, Facts, and Anecdotes for Fans of the Orange and Black.

# MY TEN FAVORITE
# FLYERS OF ALL TIME

Thousands of players that have worn the orange and black; I have watched, examined, and researched them for over thirty years. I have attempted to absorb as much information about my favorite team as possible and, consequently, I've learned to have a few favorite players. The list below includes ten talented men, but I'm definitely missing more than a few Flyer greats.

### 10. RICK TOCCHET

Rick Tocchet personified Flyers' hockey like no other player in the team's history. He was tough and abrasive -- he would drop his gloves at an instant. Tocchet twice scored forty or more goals in a single season with the Flyers and played in two Stanley Cup Finals.

### 9. MIKE RICHARDS

Though Richards is only in his fourth season with the Flyers, he has already captured the hearts of the fans - and a spot on this list. In 2007, Richards signed a contract that would keep him in Philadelphia until 2014. His combination of offensive flair, toughness and leadership has critics comparing him to the great Bobby Clarke. Richards' composure - both on- and off-ice - will make him a crowd favorite for years to come.

# FLYER'D UP!

Trivia, Facts, and Anecdotes for Fans of the Orange and Black.

### 8. MARK HOWE

As perhaps the greatest defenseman in Flyers' history, Howe had great blood lines. His offensive output in 1985-86 (while at the same time playing stellar defense) was amazing: 24 goals and 58 assists for 82 points; he finished the season with a plus/minus of plus 85. Shockingly, he never lifted the Norris Trophy; more importantly, however, the great player never hoisted the Stanley Cup -- a feat every great player, like Howe, should have the chance to do.

*Flyers captain Dave Poulin hoisting the Prince of Wales Trophy after defeating the Quebec Nordiques in 1985*

### 7. DAVE POULIN

Considered one of the best captains in team history, Poulin turned in a remarkable career for his 5'11 stature. Poulin had a desire to win while playing hurt. Wearing a flak jacket underneath his sweater to protect his cracked ribs, Poulin scored perhaps the biggest goal of his career. With the Flyers down two men versus the Quebec Nordiques in Game 6 of the 1985 Wales Conference Finals, Poulin scored on a shorthanded breakaway sending the Spectrum crowd into a crazed frenzy and the Flyers into the Stanley Cup Finals. Poulin was a true leader and model Flyer.

*Did you know that Lou Angotti was the first captain in Flyers history?*

### 6. JEREMY ROENICK

Roenick came to town like so many other free agents: he had romantic visions of winning the Stanley Cup, but left empty-handed. However, he was still one of the most popular Flyers of his era. His goal at 7:39 of the first overtime in Game 6 of the 2004 Eastern Conference Semifinals against the Toronto Maple Leafs catapulted the team to yet another Conference final appearance; to this day, it is my favorite goal in Flyers' history.

### 5. ERIC LINDROS

Lindros was labeled "The Next One". With Lindros came not only a talented player, but also amazing expectations and extreme disappointment. He nearly succeeded in achieving his goal for a Stanley Cup in 1997, but was swept in four games by the Detroit Red Wings. His time in Philadelphia was tainted by family interference, a long-standing feud with General Manager Bob Clarke, and multiple concussions for eight seasons. No Flyer ever had the physical strength, hands or hockey ability that could match those of number 88. Lindros was fun to watch. If only he could have kept his head up.

*Flyers captain Eric Lindros awaits his opponent*

### 4. RON HEXTALL

"Hexy" was the first goaltender in NHL history to score a goal on December 7, 1987 against the Boston Bruins. Later, he would accomplish that feat

# FLYER'D UP!

Trivia, Facts, and Anecdotes for Fans of the Orange and Black.

again in a 1989 playoff game versus the Washington Capitals. Hextall will forever be lauded as a fan favorite for his toughness, his grit and his desire to back his teammates. His 1987 rookie season was phenomenal; though the Flyers were eventually beaten in seven games by the Edmonton Oilers in a thrilling Stanley Cup Final, the edgy rookie goaltender earned the Vezina trophy as the league's best net-minder and the Conn Smythe trophy as the playoff MVP. Hextall somehow failed to win the Calder trophy (which went to the King's Luc Robitaille) as the league's best rookie.

### 3. PELLE LINDBERGH

Lindbergh's life was cut short during the early morning hours of November 10, 1985 as a result of a terrible automobile mobile accident. The news of his death shook me so hard, I felt as though I had lost a member of my family. In the 1984-85 season, Lindbergh led the Flyers to the Stanley Cup Finals while winning the Vezina Trophy as the first European goaltender ever to do so. During his acceptance speech at the NHL Awards ceremony, he thanked his boyhood idol and mentor, Bernie Parent. I will forever remember not only Lindbergh's words and actions, but also his character.

### 2. PETER ZEZEL

Zezel was great on face-offs and a good goalscorer. He was a young gun the Flyers had on their roster in the 1984-85 season; Zezel joined Rick Tocchet and Derek Smith as three of the

*The Flyers Peter Zezel in game action*

new faces on a very young squad led by head coach Mike Keenan. I remember Zezel for a few things: his playoff hat trick in April of '86 against the New York Rangers, his ability to use his professional soccer experience to kick the puck back to the point on face-offs, his small role in the 1986 hockey classic Youngblood and his professionalism and compassion to a pimply-faced, impressionable teenager at the 1985 Flyers Wives Fight For Lives Carnival. Zezel signed his autograph, took a picture and shook my hand. Who says athletes aren't role models?

*Reggie Leach posing with the Conn Smythe Trophy after scoring 19 goals in the 1976 Stanley Cup Playoffs.*

## 1. REGGIE LEACH

My favorite Flyer as a boy, Leach was known for his incredible slap shot that earned him the nickname "The Rifle." Leach's 1976 playoff season was my indoctrination to Flyers hockey. His 19 goals during the post season won him the Conn Smythe trophy, even though the Flyers were swept by Montreal, which ended the team's bid for three straight Cups. The "LCB line" of Leach, Bobby Clarke and Bill Barber was one of hockey's best. I never stopped trying to emulate his slap shot; I never succeeded, but it sure was fun trying.

**My Ten Favorite Flyers of All Time**

*Did you know that Rick MacLeish was the first Flyers to score 50 goals in a single season?*

# FLYER'D UP!

## 80's TRIVIA

1. Who was the first Flyers' goalie to save an opposing penalty shot?
A. Ron Hextall    B. Rick St. Croix    C. Pete Peeters    D. Pelle Lindbergh

2. Who scored the first overtime game-winning goal in Flyers history?
A. Bobby Clarke    B. Ilkka Sinisalo    C. Tim Kerr    D. Dave Poulin

3. Who holds the Flyers record for most assists in a playoff year?
A. Rick Tocchet    B. Pelle Eklund    C. Brian Propp    D. Bobby Clarke

4. Prior to the 2008-09 season, who was the last Flyer to amass more than 300 penalty minutes in one season?
A. Glen Cochrane    B. Rick Tocchet    C. Craig Berube    D. Paul Holmgren

5. Who holds the Flyers record for the fastest two goals scored by one player, scoring twice in eight seconds?
A. Ron Sutter    B. Derek Smith    C. Ilkka Sinisalo    D. Ron Flockhart

6. Who registered the most career hat tricks against the Flyers with six?
A. Mike Bossy    B. Mario Lemieux    C. Wayne Gretzky    D. Bryan Trottier

7. Who scored the game-winning goal in overtime of Game 1 of the 1987 Wales Conference Finals against Montreal?
A. Derek Smith    B. Brian Propp    C. Ilkka Sinisalo    D. Scott Mellanby

8. Who holds the Flyers record for points by a rookie defenseman with 49?
A. Behn Wilson    B. Thomas Eriksson    C. Gord Murphy    D. Kerry Huffman

9. Who was the lowest draft pick in the 1980s to make the Flyers as an everyday player?
A. Dave Brown    B. Pelle Eklund    C. Gord Murphy    D. Murray Baron

10. Rick Tocchet led the Flyers in penalty minutes in the 1980s. Who was second?
A. Craig Berube    B. Glen Cochrane    C. Paul Holmgren    D. Brad Marsh

34

**answers on page 179**

# FLYER'D UP!

Trivia, Facts, and Anecdotes for Fans of the Orange and Black.

## 80's TRIVIA

11. As of the start of the 2008-09 hockey season, the Flyers have not won a hockey game in which city since 1988?
A. St. Louis    B. Edmonton    C. Chicago    D. Detroit

12. As of the start of the 2008-09 hockey season, the Flyers have not lost a hockey game in which city since 1989?
A. Vancouver    B. Calgary    C. Los Angeles    D. Edmonton

13. Against which team did the Flyers register the highest percentage of possible points available (74.3 percent) in the 1980s?
A. Winnipeg    B. Toronto    C. Pittsburgh    D. St. Louis

14. Who scored the fastest opening goal in Flyers history (8 seconds into the game)?
A. Dave Poulin    B. Peter Zezel    C. Murray Craven    D. Tim Kerr

15. Who holds the Flyers record for goals in consecutive games with nine?
A. Brian Propp    B. Tim Kerr    C. Rick Tocchet    D. Ilkka Sinisalo

16. Three times in the 1980s the Flyers had a player score three goals in one period. Bobby Clarke and Tim Kerr were two of the players. Who was the third?
A. Murray Craven    B. Ron Flockhart    C. Ron Sutter    D. Pelle Eklund

17. What opponent holds the playoff record for most points scored in a game (eight) against the Flyers?
A. Wayne Gretzky    B. Mario Lemieux    C. Bryan Trottier    D. Mike Bossy

18. Which Flyer holds the NHL record for the fastest goal scored in a playoff game at the start of a period other than the first period (six seconds)?
A. Mark Howe    B. Doug Crossman    C. Pelle Eklund    D. Brad McCrimmon

19. Who is the only Flyer to record his first NHL goal on a penalty shot?
A. Behn Wilson    B. Dave Poulin    C. Lindsay Carson    D. Ilkka Sinisalo

**answers on page 179**

# FLYER'D UP!

## 80's TRIVIA

20. The Flyers registered a team-record 14 hat tricks in the 1984-85 season. Thirteen of them were registered by noted offensive stalwarts Tim Kerr (six), Brian Propp (four), Ilkka Sinisalo (two) and Dave Poulin (one). Who had the other?
A. Lindsay Carson     B. Derek Smith     C. Peter Zezel     D. Mark Howe

21. Which Flyers goaltender did not register a shutout between 1987 and 1990?
A. Pete Peeters     B. Mark LaForest     C. Ron Hextall     D. Ken Wregget

22. The Flyers first overtime loss came in 1984 at the Spectrum against the Buffalo Sabres. Who scored the game-winner for Buffalo?
A. Phil Housley     B. Gilbert Perrault     C. Dave Andreychuk     D. Mike Foligno

23. The first trade the Flyers made in the 1980s occurred on January 2, 1980 when they sent a bundle of cash to Vancouver for which player?
A. Ron Arehnekoff     B. Darryl Sittler     C. Norm Barnes     D. Jack McIlhargey

24. Who was the first Flyer to register 50 goals in more than one season?
A. Bill Barber     B. Tim Kerr     C. Reggie Leach     D. Bobby Clarke

25. Who shared the Jennings Trophy with Bob Froese in 1986 as the two goaltenders on the team with the lowest goals against average in the NHL?
A. Ron Hextall     B. Glen Resch     C. Darren Jensen     D. Pete Peeters

26. Which Flyers led the team in goals for the 1982-1983 season?
A) Brian Propp     B) Bobby Clarke     C) Darryl Sittler     D) Bill Barber

27. All of the following Flyers averaged more than a point per game during the 1985-1986 seasons except:
A) Brian Propp     B) Dave Poulin     C) Illka Sinisalo     D) Tim Kerr

answers on page 179

# FLYER'D UP!

Trivia, Facts, and Anecdotes for Fans of the Orange and Black.

# THE 10 GREATEST FLYERS MOMENTS AT THE SPECTRUM

### By Anthony J. SanFilippo

*Anthony J. SanFilippo covers the Flyers and the NHL for the Delaware County Daily Times. As an award-winning journalist, SanFilippo has produced work which has appeared in Sports Illustrated, on ComcastSportsNet.com and on HockeyBuzz.com.*

*Born and raised in the Overbrook section of West Philadelphia, SanFilippo is a 1991 graduate of St. Joseph's Preparatory School. He later attended college at American University in Washington, D.C. and St. Joseph's University in Philadelphia. He has also worked in Philadelphia for the Associated Press and for WIP radio.*

*He now lives in Springfield Township, Pennsylvania with his three children Anthony Jr., Amelia and Andrew.*

# FLYER'D UP!

It was a second home. There was the house in the Overbrook section of West Philadelphia where I slept every night and technically resided, but Veterans Stadium and the Spectrum were where my heart truly lived.

Those names sound refreshing in a day and age when ever-changing corporate sponsorship takes away the identities of our arenas and ballparks. Former generations had strong connections with sports complexes and their distinct personalities; current youth feel distant from their team's home stadium.

I saw some great games at the Spectrum – and some great concerts, too. Flyers' games, however, stick out more than any other event.

I wasn't at every game on this list. I was in attendance for about half of the games listed below; believe me, they were so special that I can still tell the stories about what happened vividly. I can supply the sights, the sounds, and all the colors – truly, the full Spectrum.

The building - my second home - will be missed.

● Flyers defeat Boston 1-0 to win their first Stanley Cup, May 19, 1974 – The May game marks an obviously great moment. The victory was the only professional championship won in the building by a home team. It took a Bernie Parent shutout of the big, bad Bruins to make it happen.

*The Flyers and their fans celebrate their first Stanley up, May 19th, 1974 on Spectrum ice*

**The 10 Greatest Flyers Moments at the Spectrum**

*Did you know that the Flyers were the only NHL team to defeat the Soviet Union's Central Red Army during the Soviet Series of 1976?*

# FLYER'D UP!

Trivia, Facts, and Anecdotes for Fans of the Orange and Black.

● Flyers defeat the Soviet Red Army team 4-1 on national television, January 11, 1976 – The Soviets went through the first seven games of a tour against NHL squads unbeaten. They insisted they were the best team in the world. Then, the Red Army arrived in Philadelphia. Ed Van Impe chased his opponent from the ice with a brutal check; even though they came back, the Soviets were never the same. Dave Poulin, who didn't arrive in Philadelphia until seven years later, said that the Flyers "chased Communism out of the country that day".

● Flyers defeat Edmonton 3-2 in Game 6 of the Stanley Cup Finals, May 28, 1987 – For the third time in a series against arguably the greatest hockey team ever assembled, the Flyers overcame a two-goal deficit to win and force a Game 7. Brian Propp tied the game with a power play goal in the third period; then, J.J. Daigneault secured the victory on a slapper from the point with 5:32 remaining in the game.

● Flyers defeat Quebec 3-0 in Game 6 of the Wales Conference Finals, May 16, 1985 – The victory sent the Flyers to the Finals for the fifth time in 11 seasons. It was highlighted by one of the greatest goals in Flyers history; Dave Poulin's score while the Flyers were two men short. Poulin put a breakaway goal over Mario Gosselin's glove to lock up the win. Flyers defeat Minnesota 3-2 in Game 5 of quarterfinals, April 10, 1973

● The Flyers didn't win the series against Minnesota in Game 5, but the match contained perhaps the most important goal in the franchise's history. Gary Dornhoefer made a dash from one end of the ice to the other and flipped the puck past Minnesota goalie Cesare Maniago to give the Flyers the win in overtime. The goal marked the first time the Flyers had taken a lead in a playoff series and is memorialized in a bronze statue outside the Spectrum.

**The 10 Greatest Flyers Moments at the Spectrum**

# FLYER'D UP!

Trivia, Facts, and Anecdotes for Fans of the Orange and Black.

● Flyers defeat Washington 5-4 in Game 4 of the Patrick Division semi-finals, April 10, 1988 – In one of the greatest comeback victories in NHL playoff history, the Flyers overcame a 4-1 deficit with less than 10 minutes remaining. The Philadelphia team then won the game in overtime on a goal by Murray Craven. The victory gave the Flyers a 3-1 series lead. Unfortunately, they lost the next three games and bowed out of the playoffs.

● Flyers defeat Boston 5-2, as Ron Hextall becomes the first goalie to score a goal, December 8, 1987 – Hextall had a flair for the dramatic, so it only made sense that he becomes the first NHL goalie to score a goal. He later repeated his performance in the playoffs (1989) when he also scored in Washington.

● Flyers defeat the New York Islanders 4-1 in Game 7 of the semifinals to return to the Stanley Cup Finals for the second straight season, May 13, 1975 – The Flyers dominated the game from start to finish after letting the Isles back into the series with sloppy performances in Games 5 and 6. Kate Smith made a notable return to sing "God Bless America." It was Smith's third live performance at the Spectrum and, after the Flyers won, there was no doubt that she was their good luck charm.

● Flyers defeat Pittsburgh 5-4 in Mario Lemieux's first game back after battle with cancer, March 2, 1993 – The game was inconsequential – the Flyers were a bad team, anyway; however, after the game ended, when Lemieux was named one of the stars of the game for scoring a goal and an assist, he received a lengthy standing ovation from the Flyers crowd in one of the classiest moments by fans in the sports history. Lemieux played that night after receiving his final radiation treatment earlier that morning.

# FLYER'D UP!

Trivia, Facts, and Anecdotes for Fans of the Orange and Black.

● Flyers defeat Montreal 4-3 in Game 1 of the Wales Conference Finals, May 4, 1987 – The game against Montreal was one of my personal favorites. I, wearing a Ilkka Sinisalo jersey, sat along the goal line at the Spectrum for my first playoff when I was 13. I was with my aunt, Amelia Ruffo, who was only 28 at the time. She loved the Flyers and got the tickets for the big game at last minute. It was an intense back-and-forth contest with the Canadiens ahead by a goal the whole game. Then, Derek Smith tied the match to force overtime. The game-winner then occurred right in front of me when Sinisalo (my then favorite player) poked the puck through a scrum in front of the net. My aunt and I jumped up and hugged in wild celebration. It was an emotionally draining game, but it had the perfect ending. Sinisalo had also scored earlier in the game, which made the night all the more memorable to me. It was the only hockey game I would ever attend with my aunt. Soon after, she became sick and three months after Lemieux's inspiring return to hockey, she died after a long battle with cancer at the age of 35. Part of her memory still lives on to this day thanks to a great Flyers' game at the Spectrum.

## MOST GOALS IN A GAME AT THE SPECTRUM

### Regular Season
Flyer:  4 goals, many players
(most recently by Rick Tocchet vs. WPG on 1/25/90)
Opponent:  6 goals, Red Berenson (STL, on 11/7/68)

### Playoffs
Flyer: 5 goals, Reggie Leach (vs. BOS, on 5/6/76)
Opponent: 3 goals, Jim Pappin (CHI, on 4/11/71) and Brian Leetch (NYR, on 5/22/95)

The 10 Greatest Flyers Moments at the Spectrum  41

*Did you know that the Flyers were the first and one of only two teams to ever wear long pants (the other being the Hartford Whalers) in the NHL? They did so for two seasons in 1981-82 and 1982-83.*

## MOST GOALS AS A FLYER AT THE SPECTRUM

### Regular Season
231 Barber, Bill
209 Kerr, Tim
191 Clarke, Bobby

### Playoffs
36 MacLeish, Rick
34 Barber, Bill
29 Leach, Reggie

## MOST GOALS AS A FLYERS' OPPONENT AT THE SPECTRUM

### Regular Season
21 Lemieux, Mario
20 Esposito, Phil
19 Trottier, Bryan

### Playoffs
8 Maloney, Don
6 Potvin, Denis
6 Duguay, Ron

# FLYER'D UP!

Trivia, Facts, and Anecdotes for Fans of the Orange and Black.

## PENALTY SHOTS AT THE SPECTRUM
### (Regular Season)

| Date | TEAM | -FINAL SCORE- | Result | Goalie |
|------|------|---------------|--------|--------|
| 01/31/1974 Rick Martin | BUF | PHI 4 vs BUF 3 | Goal | Parent, Bernie |
| 03/07/1974 Bill Clement | PHI | PHI 6 vs DET 1 | No G | Rutherford, Jim |
| 11/09/1974 Orest Kindrachuk | PHI | PHI 6 vs WAS 2 | Goal | Belhumeur, Michel |
| 03/20/1978 Rick MacLeish | PHI | PHI 4 vs NYI 2 | Goal | Smith, Billy |
| 10/14/1979 Lanny McDonald | TOR | PHI 4 vs TOR 3 | Goal | Peeters, Pete |
| 10/11/1981 Ilkka Sinisalo | PHI | PHI 8 vs PIT 2 | Goal | Harrison, Paul |
| 12/17/1981 Behn Wilson | PHI | PHI 2 vs BUF 1 | Goal | Edwards, Don |
| 11/18/1982 Lanny McDonald | CGY | PHI 3 vs CGY 2 | No G | Lindbergh, Pelle |
| 01/04/1983 Brian Propp | PHI | PHI 4 vs VAN 1 | Goal | Ellacott, Ken |
| 11/03/1984 Scott Bjugstad | DAL | PHI 5 vs MIN 1 | No G | Lindbergh, Pelle |
| 11/18/1984 Ron Sutter | PHI | PHI 3 vs NYI 3 | No G | Hrudey, Kelly |
| 12/19/1985 Brian Propp | PHI | PHI 6 vs NJ 3 | No G | Resch, Chico |
| 03/06/1986 Dave Poulin | PHI | PHI 7 vs TOR 4 | No G | Edwards, Don |
| 01/06/1987 Rick Tocchet | PHI | PHI 4 vs NJ 0 | No G | Billington, Craig |
| 10/24/1987 Jan Erixon | NYR | PHI 3 vs NYR 5 | Goal | LaForest, Mark |
| 03/12/1988 Mark Johnson | NJ | PHI 5 vs NJ 6 | Goal | Hextall, Ron |
| 12/23/1990 Murray Craven | PHI | PHI 4 vs MTL 4 | Goal | Racicot, Andre |
| 02/05/1991 Normand Lacombe | PHI | PHI 2 vs LA 3 | Goal | Hrudey, Kelly |
| 10/13/1991 Murray Craven | PHI | PHI 4 vs NJ 2 | No G | Terreri, Chris |
| 11/23/1991 Doug Brown | NJ | PHI 5 vs NJ 5 | Goal | Wregget, Ken |

*Did you know that no penalty shots were attempted in the playoffs at the Spectrum?*

# FLYER'D UP!

## 90's TRIVIA

1. Prior to Glen Metropolit in the 2008-09 season, who was the only Flyers *regular* to wear number 13 on his jersey?
A. Petr Svoboda   B. Mike Ricci   C. Yves Racine   D. Claude Lapointe

2. Who holds the record for most shutouts against the Flyers with eight?
A. Martin Brodeur   B. Dominik Hasek   C. Patrick Roy   D. John Vanbiesbrouck

3. Who has the lowest career playoff goals against average of any Flyers goalie who started at least six playoff games?
A. Roman Cechmanek   B. Bernie Parent   C. John Vanbiesbrouck   D. Ron Hextall

4. Who holds the Flyers rookie record for points in a season?
A. Dave Poulin   B. Ron Flockhart   C. Eric Lindros   D. Mikael Renberg

5. Who has won the most Bobby Clarke trophies in recognition of being named the Flyers' MVP?
A. Mark Recchi   B. Eric Lindros   C. Ron Hextall   D. John LeClair

6. Who was the last Flyer to be named a first team NHL All-Star at the end of a season?
A. Eric Lindros   B. Eric Desjardins   C. John LeClair   D. Ron Hextall

7. The Flyers have only drafted two goalies in the first round in team history. Who was the first?
A. Jean-Marc Pelletier   B. Brian Boucher   C. Roman Cechmanek   D. Maxime Ouellet

8. In 2008, Mike Richards scored the second penalty shot playoff goal in Flyers' history. Who scored the first?
A. Eric Lindros   B. Valeri Zelepukin   C. Eric Desjardins   D. Mark Recchi

9. In 1992-93, the Flyers had eight hat tricks. Eric Lindros, Rod Brind'Amour and Kevin Dineen had seven of them. Who had the eighth?
A. Brent Fedyk   B. Garry Galley   C. Vyacheslav Butsayev   D. Greg Paslawski

44

answers on page 179

# FLYER'D UP!

Trivia, Facts, and Anecdotes for Fans of the Orange and Black.

## 90's TRIVIA

10. Who is the only player who played at least one game for the 1990-91 Flyers that was still on a professional hockey roster at the start of the 2008-09 season?
A. Darren Rumble    B. Mark Pederson    C. Kimbi Daniels    D. Mike Ricci

11. Which goalie, who started at least 10 games for the Flyers, has the lowest goals against average in franchise history?
A. Roman Cechmanek    B. John Vanbiesbrouck    C. Brian Boucher    D. Garth Snow

12. When the Flyers returned to the playoffs for the first time in six years in 1995, they had three consecutive overtimes decided on goals by defensemen. Who scored the first overtime game-winner?
A. Eric Desjardins    B. Karl Dykhuis    C. Kevin Haller    D. Petr Svoboda

13. In the '90s, the Flyers set a franchise record for most shots on goal in one period of a playoff game with 28. Who was their opponent?
A. New Jersey Devils          B. Pittsburgh Penguins
C. Tampa Bay Lightning        D. Florida Panthers

14. Who registered the only postseason hat trick against the Flyers in the 1990s?
A. Claude Lemieux    B. Patrik Elias    C. Brendan Shanahan    D. Wayne Gretzky

15. In the 1990s, who was the only player to lead the Flyers in penalty minutes for more than one season?
A. Terry Carkner    B. Eric Lindros    C. Shawn Antoski    D. Dan Kordic

16. The Flyers had a string of nine consecutive seasons where either Mark Recchi, Eric Lindros or John LeClair led the team in scoring. Who was the last player to lead the team prior to that dynamic trio?
A. Rod Brind'Amour    B. Rick Tocchet    C. Kevin Dineen    D. Pelle Eklund

17. Who was the last Flyer to score three goals in one period?
A. Eric Lindros    B. Mikael Renberg    C. John LeClair    D. Murray Craven

45

answers on page 179

# FLYER'D UP!

## 90's TRIVIA

18. Who holds the Flyers record for longest shutout streak at 227:04?
A. Ron Hextall     B. John Vanbiesbrouck     C. Garth Snow     D. Dominic Roussel

19. Who was the Flyers leading scorer on defense in 1990-91?
A. Gord Murphy     B. Terry Carkner     C. Mark Howe     D. Jiri Latal

20. Who was the Flyers top-scoring right winger in 1998-99?
A. Trent Klatt     B. Jody Hull     C. Mikael Renberg     D. Keith Jones

21. What coach of a 2008-09 NHL team finished his NHL playing career with the Flyers in the 1990s?
A. Terry Murray     B. John Stevens     C. Dave Tippett     D. Craig Hartsburg

22. Who played for the Flyers in parts of two seasons in the 1990s and later went on to coach at Princeton University?
A. Bruce Hoffort     B. Pat Falloon     C. Kevin Haller     D. Andre Faust

23. Who was the oldest Flyers draft pick still on an NHL roster at the completion of the 2007-08 season?
A. Chris Therien     B. Vaclav Prospal     C. Peter Forsberg     D. Janne Niinimaa

24. Aside from Simon Gagne, who is the only other player on the Flyers 2008-09 roster who was originally drafted by the team in the 1990s?
A. Mike Knuble     B. Antero Niittymaki     C. Ossi Vaananen     D. Arron Asham

25. Who posted the first hat trick of the 1996-97 season for the Flyers, the only three-goal game of his Flyers' career?
A. Dale Hawerchuk     B. Trent Klatt     C. Shjon Podein     D. Joel Otto

26. During which NHL season did Eric Lindros record his only 100 point season?
A) 1994-1995     B) 1995-1996     C) 1996-1997     D) 1997-1998

**answers on page 179**

# FLYER'D UP!

Trivia, Facts, and Anecdotes for Fans of the Orange and Black.

## FLYERS GOALTENDERS WORD SEARCH

```
U E S T M T R K A M P R K C N
I M N O O E S C H E N O R I B
B K O B E L H U M E U R E N S
I R A R T G B O U C H E R N J
E S E M T S E R O F A L O E H
P C T H Y S T B G I C W N S C
N E H E G T R S S W K S I S S
U T E E P R T E G G E R W E E
W U X T C H E I D N T O T F R
O T T I E H E B I O T U E F P
S E A F O R M N D N S S K A R
A A L Y Y R S A S N E S R V I
H T L M L K C V N O I E U E N
E H O F F O R T R E N L B L H
G A M B L E R F S T K R T L W
```

| | | |
|---|---|---|
| HEXTALL | PARENT | STEPHENSON |
| FROESE | CHECHMANEK | LINDBERGH |
| PEETERS | FAVELL | ROUSSEL |
| ESCHE | NIITTYMAKI | VANBIESBROUCK |
| BIRON | BOUCHER | WREGGET |
| SNOW | STCROIX | SODERSTROM |
| MYRE | JENSEN | TAYLOR |
| BURKE | HACKETT | GAMBLE |
| LAFOREST | BELHUMEUR | RESCH |
| HOFFORT | MOORE | INNESS |

47

**answers on page 182**

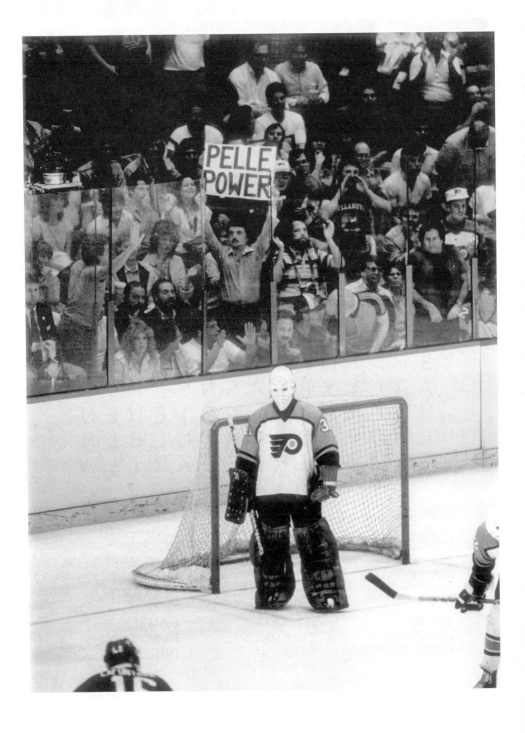

# REMEMBERING PELLE LINDBERGH
## By Bill Meltzer

*Bill Meltzer covers Flyers alumni topics for Philadelphiaflyers.com and international hockey for NHL.com and IIHF.com. He is also the primary Flyers blogger for Hockeybuzz. com. A lifelong Philadelphia resident, Meltzer went to George Washington High School and Temple University. Today, he lives in the city with wife Laura.*

The phone rang early on the morning of Sunday, November 10, 1985. It was David Kramer, one of my closest childhood friends. We went different high schools but still talked about sports -- especially hockey -- and got together from time to time.

We had just talked the previous evening following the Flyers' victory over the Boston Bruins, which brought the Philadelphia team's winning streak to 10. Dave and I had discussed his plans to spend the weekend at his family's house at the Jersey shore. Our conversation was light-hearted.

I wasn't immediately sure why David was calling. On occasion, he would bring me along to Flyers games with his family; however, we hadn't made plans for any upcoming games, so it was a strange time for a call.

"Did you hear about Pelle?" he asked almost immediately.
"Pelle Lindbergh?"
"Yeah."
"What about him?"
"Turn on the TV," he replied.
"OK. What channel?"

# FLYER'D UP!

Trivia, Facts, and Anecdotes for Fans of the Orange and Black.

"Any channel."

I flipped on the television. One of the local stations had a live report about a devastating car crash involving the Vezina Trophy-winning goaltender. Lindbergh had driven his customized Porsche 930 Turbo into a wall after failing to negotiate a steep curve in Somerdale, New Jersey.

Lindbergh had been declared brain dead, and could breathe only with the assistance of a respirator. The two passengers in his car had suffered serious injuries. Lindbergh's family elected that the respirator be turned off and his organs donated to patients in need of transplants.

Flyers coach Mike Keenan called it Pelle's final - and greatest - save.

Like countless other Flyers' fans around the Delaware Valley, Lindbergh's death hits me hard. At 26, he had every reason to live.

Lindbergh was already the best goaltender in the NHL. His team was the youngest in the NHL but was a legitimate contender for the Stanley Cup. The club made it to the Finals the previous year, and looked even better in the early going of the 1985-86 season.

Most importantly, he was an extremely well-liked player; he was a decent human being with an omnipresent smile, a legion of friends and fans and a beautiful fiancée whom he planned to marry after the season.

In the days after the crash, tests revealed that Lindbergh had a blood alcohol level far above the legal limit when he got behind the wheel of his Porsche after leaving a team party at the Coliseum in Voorhees, New Jersey (the team's practice facility, which also featured an after-hours bar).

 **Remembering Pelle Lindbergh**

*Did you know that the Flyers did not have a captain for the 1992-93 season?*

# FLYER'D UP!

Trivia, Facts, and Anecdotes for Fans of the Orange and Black.

Those who (even casually) knew Lindbergh were shocked to hear that he died as a result of drinking and driving. He rarely drank during the hockey season but, after a busy stretch of games, the team had five days until its next match. He allowed himself to indulge more than he normally would, although eyewitnesses swore that Lindbergh did not seem to be significantly impaired when he left the Coliseum.

Unfortunately, no one was surprised that the accident involved Lindbergh driving at dangerous speeds. Lindbergh often drove like he was trying out for Nascar. He laughed off repeated warnings from friends and family.
The real lesson of Lindbergh's death is not just that drinking and driving don't mix. It's that life is fragile and should never be taken for granted. Lindbergh was a gentle and caring human being. The last thing he'd have ever wanted to do would be to hurt his parents, fiancée, teammates, friends and fans. He loved life but threw away his own; he left everyone to cope with the grief and the pain.

Lindbergh came from a working-class family of salt-of-the-earth people. He got his gregarious nature from his mother, Anna-Lisa. From his late father, Sigge, he got his love of sports and deep commitment to his loved ones. The Lindbergh family went through a level of pain that no parent should ever experience. In 1985, they buried Pelle. Less than two years later, they buried his older sister, Ann-Christine, who went through a multi-year ordeal of battling cancer only to see it return and claim her life.

Lindbergh was also blessed to have a fiancée, Kerstin, who was as devoted and loving as she was beautiful. The two were a great match -- they balanced each other perfectly. Kerstin was the practical one; Pelle was the dreamer.

# FLYER'D UP!

Trivia, Facts, and Anecdotes for Fans of the Orange and Black.

No player in Flyers' history, from Bobby Clarke to Simon Gagne, was more proud to wear the Flyers' uniform than Pelle Lindbergh. During a time in Sweden when few people followed the NHL, Lindbergh made it his goal at age 10 to play in the League. He even adopted the Flyers as his favorite team long before he was ever drafted.

At first, his interest was superficial. He liked the Flyers logo and would sometimes doodle it in his composition book at school, rather than paying attention in class. When he took a trip to Canada with his youth hockey team in 1971, Pelle bought a Flyers jersey in a Toronto sporting goods store. In 1974, he discovered Bernie Parent.

At the end of each season, Lindbergh's youth coach hosted a get-together for the kids in the program. During the party, he showed an 8 mm film of the Stanley Cup Finals. Lindbergh was mesmerized by Flyers goalie Bernie Parent, who won both the Vezina Trophy as the NHL's top goaltender and the Conn Smythe Trophy as playoff MVP.

Lindbergh became consumed by Parent and the Flyers. He purchased the same brands of equipment as Parent and patterned his stand-up style of goaltending after the legendary Flyer. He even bought a Parent replica mask, on which he also put Flyers' decals. Lindbergh showed his pride in the organization by sporting the team logo in international competitions as well as Swedish league games.

Lindbergh was open about the fact that his goal was to not only play in the NHL, but also to play for the team of his idol. When Lindbergh was drafted by the Flyers in 1979, he was living his own dream.

After his retirement as a player, Parent became the Flyers' goaltending

# FLYER'D UP!

Trivia, Facts, and Anecdotes for Fans of the Orange and Black.

coach. He and Lindbergh formed a unique bond that went beyond a typical coach-player relationship. Lindbergh often called Parent his "dad in the USA," as their friendship had a paternalistic quality.

Watching Lindbergh blossom into the best goaltender in the NHL was almost like seeing Bernie Parent in his prime reborn in another goalie's body. The similarities were almost eerie.

That Lindbergh died in a drunk driving accident almost had an ironic undertone to it. After Parent's playing career ended due to a serious eye injury, he spiraled downhill into alcoholism. Only after regaining control of his life was Parent able to become the coach and man who helped Lindbergh win the 1984-85 Vezina Trophy and lead the Flyers to the Stanley Cup Finals. There wasn't a dry eye in the ballroom when Lindbergh accepted the Vezina Trophy and thanked his friend and mentor.

The Flyers were a close-knit team before Lindbergh's death. Part of their bond lay in having tyrannical head coach Mike Keenan as a common enemy. But the locker room had almost a perfect blend of personalities as well tremendous talent and depth on the ice.

The club had an extraordinary captain in Dave Poulin and just the right number of seasoned leaders -- in particular, defensemen Mark Howe and Brad Marsh -- to balance the youthful exuberance of players like Rick Tocchet, Murray Craven and Peter Zezel. Lindbergh was universally well-liked in the locker room. He didn't have the stereotypically aloof and intense goaltender's personality.

After Lindbergh's death, the team grew even closer. Focusing on hockey was a respite from the pain of coping with the loss of their friend and teammate.

# FLYER'D UP!

Trivia, Facts, and Anecdotes for Fans of the Orange and Black.

In the first game after the crash, the team downed the defending champion Edmonton Oilers, 5-3. By the end of the season, Philly racked up 110 points to win the Patrick Division.

But Pelle's death put goaltender Bob Froese in an untenable position. No matter what Froese did, he was unfavorably compared to Lindbergh. Even after Froese won the Jennings Trophy (lowest goals against average) during the regular season, he was considered the team's weakest link. When he was named to the All-Star team at midseason, Keenan paid him a backhanded compliment by saying that Froese's "statistics justify his selection".

Nevertheless, the Flyers entered their first round playoff series against the New York Rangers as a prohibitive favorite. The Flyers finished 22 points ahead of the hated "Blue Shirts" during the regular season. Philly's lineup was healthier than it had been the previous spring, and its nucleus was already battle-tested from the run to the 1985 Finals and the aftermath of Lindbergh's death.

Goaltending, however, is the sport's great equalizer. Froese was a good goaltender, but the Rangers too had a great goalie -- John Vanbiesbrouck, who won the 1985-86 Vezina Trophy en route to building career worthy of Hall of Fame induction. Vanbiesbrouck stole two games of the series, while Froese made some costly mistakes. The Flyers lost their composure, and lost the best-of-five series, three games to two.

Would the Flyers have won the 1985-86 Stanley Cup if Lindbergh had lived? They may have, although Froese was hardly the lone culprit in the loss to the Rangers. The Oilers were dominated by the Calgary Flames in the second round of the playoffs; eventual champion Montreal took out Calgary in five games in the Finals. Even with Froese, the Flyers were capable of

# FLYER'D UP!

Trivia, Facts, and Anecdotes for Fans of the Orange and Black.

going all the way if the matchups broke in their favor. Had Lindbergh lived, everything would have been in place for a Philadelphia championship.

The following season, rookie goaltender Ron Hextall burst onto the scene and led the Flyers back to the Finals; he took Edmonton to the brink before losing in Game 7. It's hard to imagine that even Lindbergh could have topped Hextall's phenomenal season, in which he won both the Vezina and Conn Smythe Trophies.

After the 1986-87season, the Flyers went quickly backward. The players mutinied against Keenan. Injuries to Mark Howe and Tim Kerr kept two key players out of the lineup for long stretches, while Hextall struggled with a series of groin pulls and was unable to match his rookie performance. General manager Bob Clarke compounded the problem with ill-advised trades and poor drafts. In 1989-90, the Flyers missed the playoffs for the first of what would become five consecutive years.

But wins and losses on the ice aren't what ultimately count. That awful night in November was among the most horrific and traumatic losses the Flyers family has ever suffered. The organization and its fans would never be the same.

**Remembering Pelle Lindbergh**

*Did you know that no Flyers player has worn jersey #31 since the death of Flyers goaltender Pelle Lindbergh in 1985?*

## 2000's TRIVIA

1. Entering the 2008-09 season, to which team have the Flyers never lost on the road?
A. Columbus Blue Jackets
B. Nashville Predators
C. Atlanta Thrashers
D. Minnesota Wild

2. Of the teams the Flyers have played more than once in the postseason, which two teams have they have never beaten in a series?
A. Chicago and Edmonton
B. Ottawa and St. Louis
C. Ottawa and Edmonton
D. St. Louis and Chicago

3. Who is the only player to wear five different uniform numbers while playing for the Flyers?
A. Stefan Ruzicka
B. Alexandre Picard
C. Patrick Sharp
D. Mark Greig

4. When the Flyers finished with their worst record in franchise history in 2006-07, who was the only other player besides 40-goal scorer Simon Gagne to register 20 goals?
A. Jeff Carter
B. Mike Knuble
C. Peter Forsberg
D. R. J. Umberger

5. How many members of the 2004-2005 Calder Cup-winning Philadelphia Phantoms played for the Flyers in 2005-06?
A. 8
B. 11
C. 14
D. 17

6. Who scored the only goal for the Flyers in Game 6 of the 2000 Eastern Conference Finals against New Jersey?
A. John LeClair
B. Keith Primeau
C. Andy Delmore
D. Eric Lindros

7. Who scored the overtime game-winner for the Flyers in Game 6 of the 2004 Eastern Conference Finals against Tampa Bay?
A. Jeremy Roenick
B. Keith Primeau
C. Mark Recchi
D. Simon Gagne

8. Who scored the overtime game-winner for the Flyers in Game 4 of the 2004 Eastern Conference semifinals against Toronto?
A. Jeremy Roenick
B. Keith Primeau
C. Mark Recchi
D. Simon Gagne

56

# FLYER'D UP!

Trivia, Facts, and Anecdotes for Fans of the Orange and Black.

## 2000's TRIVIA

9. Who scored the overtime game-winner for the Flyers in Game 6 of the 2004 Eastern Conference Finals against Toronto?
A. Jeremy Roenick          B. Keith Primeau
C. Mark Recchi             D. Simon Gagne

10. What defenseman led the Flyers is blocked shots during the 2007-08 season?
A. Derian Hatcher          B. Lasse Kukkonen
C. Jason Smith             D. Randy Jones

11. Who led the Flyers in scoring in the 2005-06 playoffs?
A. Simon Gagne             B. Mike Knuble
C. Peter Forsberg          D. Jeff Carter

12. Who holds the franchise record for the longest winless streak as a goalie?
A. Antero Niittymaki       B. Brian Boucher
C. Roman Cechmanek         D. Robert Esche

13. In John Stevens' first season as a professional head coach with the Philadelphia Phantoms, how did the team finish?
A. They missed the playoffs.          B. They won the Calder Cup.
C. They lost in the Conference Finals.          D. They lost in the Conference semifinals.

14. How many different players have been captain of the Flyers since 2000?
A. 7          B. 5          C. 4          D. 6

15. How many different coaches have the Flyers had since 2000?
A. 4          B. 6          C. 5          D. 3

16. Who did the Flyers trade to acquire the first round pick used to select Jeff Carter in 2003?
A. Andy Delmore            B. Daymond Langkow
C. Eric Lindros            D. Dan McGillis

57

**answers on page 179**

# FLYER'D UP!

Trivia, Facts, and Anecdotes for Fans of the Orange and Black.

## 2000's TRIVIA

17. How many regulars did the Flyers receive in the completed trade with Nashville for Peter Forsberg in 2007?
A. 2              B. 3              C. 4              D. 5

18. How many goals did the Flyers score in their five game opening round loss to the Ottawa Senators in the 2002 playoffs?
A. 2              B. 4              C. 5              D. 7

19. In 2002-03, his first year with the Flyers, Jeremy Roenick led the team in goals with 27. Who was second?
A. Mark Recchi              B. Michal Handzus
C. Keith Primeau           D. Simon Gagne

20. Who led the Flyers in assists in the 2006-07 season with a lowly total of 39?
A. Peter Forsberg          B. Mike Knuble
C. Simon Gagne             D. Joni Pitkanen

21. Who set the franchise record for lowest goals against average by a goalie for one season for the Flyers?
A. Brian Boucher           B. Robert Esche
C. Roman Cechmanek         D. Antero Niittymaki

22. Simon Gagne has the most career points as a Flyer on the 2007-08 opening day roster. Who is second?
A. Jeff Carter             B. Mike Richards
C. Mike Knuble             D. Scottie Upshall

23. Which team has shut out the Flyers the most since 2000 (seven times)?
Pittsburgh Penguins        B. Buffalo Sabres
C. New Jersey Devils       D. Ottawa Senators

24. Conversely, the Flyers have shutout which team the most since 2000 (five times?)
A. Buffalo Sabres          B. New York Islanders
C. Tampa Bay Lightning     D. Pittsburgh Penguins

58

**answers on page 179**

# FLYER'D UP!

Trivia, Facts, and Anecdotes for Fans of the Orange and Black.

# MEMORIES FROM THOSE WHO WORE THE ORANGE AND BLACK

The Philadelphia Flyers franchise was born in 1967. Thousands of players, wearing the proud orange and black, have walked through the doors at the Spectrum and Wachovia Canter and played the wonderful game of hockey. Fans of the team have broad memories of Flyers' history: from their entering the NHL in the 1960's; to winning the Stanley Cup in the 1970's; to playing incredible hockey in the 1980s; to transitioning and transforming during the 1990's and 2000's. The Flyers' exciting brand of hockey brought together a city by creating moments that will never be erased or forgotten.

Whether it was the groundbreaking at the Spectrum, the championship parades, the many personalities or the fantastic games, the fans of this team have had one remarkable ride. The Flyers, too, have had their share of fantastic moments: the 40-plus seasons, the road trips, the fantastic goals, the great saves, the playoffs, the triumphs and the tragedies. All of these moments -- the moments that live in the hearts of fans and players -- have combined to formulate one rich and complex history. Below are just a few of the fondest memories, which have been etched into the minds of those who gave their all for the orange and the black. Some of them are funny, some serious and some just flat out unbelievable.

# FLYER'D UP!

Trivia, Facts, and Anecdotes for Fans of the Orange and Black.

***Bob "The Hound" Kelly (1970-80)***
Bob Kelly, who was a part of both Stanley Cups, had been integral to the franchise's success in the 1970's. Though Kelly couldn't come up with just one favorite memory, he did have several fond ones. These moments, said the former Flyer, will stay with him forever.

"The first Stanley Cup was amazing; being the first expansion team to win the Cup was awesome. But, in 1976, the Soviet Series versus the Central Red Army team was [a game] for the ages."

The Flyers were the only one of four NHL teams to defeat the USSR's best. On Sunday, January 11, 1976, the Philadelphia team tallied a 4-1 victory in a game Kelly will never forget.

"The whole league hated us -- the Broad Street Bullies -- and now, here we were, trying to save the league from embarrassment. They were all with us that night. With the Cold War going on and the Kate Smith factor, and the fans were so charged up, it was just an incredible experience."

Kelly played 10 seasons in Philadelphia, during which time he had many magical memories. One of the player's favorites, however, was the parade down Broad Street. He vividly remembers an odd incident that had transpired amongst the estimated two million delighted citizens who gathered that sunny afternoon in May of 1974.

"There were just throngs of people and the city had no idea that that many

*Did you know that the Flyers all time leader in hat tricks is Tim Kerr, with 17?*

people would come out to celebrate. They had horses for crowd control and I remember a little boy got kicked in the face by one of [the horses] and had to be taken to the hospital."

The six year-old boy, Frankie Hudson of South Philadelphia was taken to Methodist Hospital.

"I remember the very next day, going to the hospital to visit [Frankie] and on my way in, Mr. Snider was coming out. He gave the child everything he could find and offered to take care of any of the outstanding hospital bills. That's the kind of guy Ed Snider is and what the Flyers are all about."

### Orest Kindrachcuk (1972-78)
"I simply remember the Delaware Valley, the entire region grabbing a hold of us and never letting go. What a wonderful road this franchise has traveled; everywhere we had gone, the fans embraced us and absolutely loved us. That is something I will never forget."

Kindrachuck's greatest playoff moment came in a deciding Game 6 of the 1975 Stanley Cup Finals versus the Buffalo Sabres. With the Flyers leading 1-0, Kindrachuk took a holding penalty which gave Buffalo their sixth power play of the game. The Sabres didn't score, but the penalty caused some good-natured ribbing from his son.

"What were you doing taking a penalty in a one-goal game with 9 minutes left?" his son had asked.

Kindrachuck shot back with this classic response:

# FLYER'D UP!

Trivia, Facts, and Anecdotes for Fans of the Orange and Black.

"When I got back to the bench after we killed that penalty, Freddie Shero gave me no lip and kept sending me out there. Then with under 3 minutes to play, both Sabres defensemen Jerry Korab and Lee Fogolin went after me and I was able to get the puck to Billy Clement. He scored and we won 2-0!"

### Gary Dornhoefer  (1967-78)
"Well, winning the Stanley Cup was the greatest memory I will ever have, but one [memory] that sticks out in my mind was one that had happened a year before."

Dornhoefer was alluding to the 1973 NHL playoffs where the Flyers had earned their very first postseason series win, four games to two over the Minnesota North Stars.  During this series, he had scored what was (at the time) the biggest goal in franchise history. In the first overtime of Game 5, he beat North Stars' goaltender Cesare Maniago at 8:35 for the 3-2 victory.  The win gave the Flyers a 3-2 series lead; they would wrap up the competition two nights later in Minnesota.

"I remember that was such a huge goal at the time, it gave us the confidence we needed."

Dornhoefer's awesome goal would later be captured in bronze forever outside the Spectrum; a statue depicting Dorny flying through the air over the fallen goaltender still stands today. Dornhoefer humbly said it was always about the team. Although the statue is certainly a great honor, the great player questioned, "You do know what pigeons do to statues, don't you?"

# FLYER'D UP!

Trivia, Facts, and Anecdotes for Fans of the Orange and Black.

The Flyers would eventually bow to the Montreal Canadiens in five tough games in the semi-finals, but it was the ovation from the Spectrum crowd prior to Game 3 after earning a split at the Forum, that was the best memory of all.

"The sound of that building when we came out on the ice was a moment I will never forget. I can remember that so distinctively; the fans were so proud that we were able to win in Montreal."

*The Flyers Mark Howe in game action during the 1985-1986 season*

### Mark Howe (1982-92)

Mark Howe, the son of the legendary Gordie Howe, recalls his time with the Flyers as the ultimate exercise in team building. The Flyers prided themselves on achieving success together -- it was the reason they had accomplished so much. The warm feelings of bonding and camaraderie remain with Howe as he fondly recalls the decade he had with the organization.

"I felt like family. I knew the organization cared about my family also. The concept of winning and hard work through team play was what was instilled in me as a young boy and it was a concept that was followed by the Flyers."

Howe, who is considered by many experts to be the best defenseman in NHL history to have never won the Norris Trophy, said the drive for the Cup was the only thing that mattered.

# FLYER'D UP!

Trivia, Facts, and Anecdotes for Fans of the Orange and Black.

"Winning as a team was the focus and individual honors were not the priority. That is the only way to enjoy success as a team."

His greatest post-season memory begins with the Flyers trailing 2-1 late in the third period during Game 6 of the 1987 Stanley Cup Finals versus Edmonton. Brian Prop then tied the game at 2 on a power play goal. Remarkably, just over a minute later, defenseman JJ Daigneault scored on a blast from the point that sent 17,222 in attendance into a cacophonous frenzy that could be heard from miles away.

"When Daigneault scored the game-winning goal, I thought the roof was going to cave in at the Spectrum because the roar of the crowd was making the building shake."

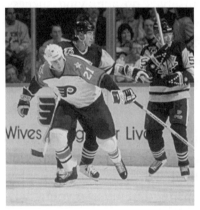

### Dave Brown (1982-85 91-95)
Like his playing style on the ice, Dave Brown has memories that are straight to the point. The rough, determined Brown stated that playing in the 1987 Stanley Cup final versus Edmonton was his fondest post-season memory. The former Philadelphia player wishes that the Cup that he won as a member of the 1990 Oilers was won with a different team - the Flyers.

"Drinking from the Cup in 1990 is my most specific memory."

"Brownie" had his chance in '85 and '87 with the Flyers, but both times the team had fallen short to the Oilers.

*Did you know that goaltender Roman Cechmanek recorded the lowest goals against average in Flyers history for a single season (playing in at least 50 games) with a stellar 1.96?*

# FLYER'D UP!

Trivia, Facts, and Anecdotes for Fans of the Orange and Black.

### Brian Propp (1979-90)

Brian Propp is among the most accomplished forwards to ever play for the orange and black. Only Bob Clarke and Bill Barber tallied more points as Flyers. Propp was critical to the team's success in the mid-eighties; he looks back on his times with the Flyers with pride.

"I remember the 35-game unbeaten streak, scoring a goal in my very first game, and playing twice for the Flyers in the Stanley Cup finals."

*The Flyers Brian Propp giving his classic "Guffaw"*

Propp played a critical role in the '87 series versus Edmonton. He recorded four assists in Game 5 and scored the tying goal in Game 6 at the Spectrum. Propp trails only Clarke on the Flyers all-time playoff scoring list. His 112 points are just seven behind Clarke, despite his playing in 20 fewer games.

### Craig Berube (1986-1991, 98-00)

Craig Berube served two different stints with the team. Known as the greatest of agitators, it is not a surprise that "The Chief" recalled one of his best bouts as one of his finest memories.

"It was very early in my career when I fought Bob Probert at the Spectrum and I made a name for myself by busting his nose. He was one tough player. I fought him twice and then a couple nights later in Detroit."

And although "The Chief" racked up an amazing 3,149 penalty minutes in

# FLYER'D UP!

Trivia, Facts, and Anecdotes for Fans of the Orange and Black.

his career, he did find time to contribute some big goals along the way. He was especially active in the post-season; Berube fondly recalls participating in the Washington Capitals Cup run in 1998 when he beat Sabres goaltender Dominik Hasek in the semi-finals. Berube's biggest playoff goal for the Flyers came in Game 4 of the 2000 Eastern Conference Finals at the Meadowlands in New Jersey to give the Flyers a 2-1 lead with just 7:02 to play in the third period.

As Berube skated back to the bench after that big goal, Flyers forward Keith Jones recalled this golden nugget:

"Here we are in such a big game and then it hits me. I leaned over to 'Chief' and I told him, 'Great job getting us the lead, but what in the world are you doing on the ice in a tie game on the road with time running out?'"

Berube flashed his famous smile and then picked up the game's first star. The playoff goal was the last one Berube would ever tally as a member of the orange and black. The Flyers would go on to win the game, but lose the series by squandering a 3-1 series lead and falling four games to three.

### Ron Hextall (1986-1992, 94-99)

Ron Hextall captured the hearts of fans during his two stints with the Flyers, during which time he personified great Flyer hockey. Hextall revolutionized the goaltending position with his great ability to handle the puck. Acting like a third defenseman, Hextall scored two goals in his playing career, the first against the Boston Bruins on December 8th, 1987. He was the first goalie to shoot the puck into the opponent's net; Hextall would repeat the feat during the following postseason in a playoff game

# FLYER'D UP!

Trivia, Facts, and Anecdotes for Fans of the Orange and Black.

against the Washington Capitals.

But for all of his stick-handing abilities and classic goaltending, Hextall was most remembered for his feisty mentality; his ability to play with raw emotion was a quality loved universally by Flyers fans, who ate Hextall up like a South Philly Cheesesteak. The Flyer faithful loved the fact that "Hexy" was willing to stick up for his teammates and to deliver exciting action every night.

During Hextall's rookie year, the Flyers went to the Stanley Cup Finals, where they eventually lost to Edmonton in a series many believe was the greatest Final ever played. Hextall won the Vezina Trophy in 1987 and the Conn Smythe Trophy for his remarkable play in the Finals. Hextall recalls the series versus Edmonton as moments that will live in his mind forever; after all, he shared it with the fans.

"1987 was fantastic. I remember after Game 6, I had to be escorted to my car outside the Spectrum like I was a rock star. I couldn't get to my car because of the throngs of fans that were just going crazy. Their passion was unbelievable. And then, when we came home in the middle of the night after losing Game 7, there were thousands of [fans] welcoming us home. I'll never forget it."

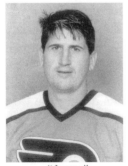
*"Jonesy"*

### Keith Jones (1998-2001)
Though Jones didn't spend much time as a Flyer, he quickly became a fan favorite. The connection Jones felt with the organization and the area remained with him long after his time in the orange and black expired -- he has now settled in the Delaware Valley and calls Philadelphia his home. His work ethic on the ice was unmatched; today, his vivid personality has allowed

# FLYER'D UP!

Trivia, Facts, and Anecdotes for Fans of the Orange and Black.

him to be the resident Flyers expert who breaks down the nightly hockey action on Comcast Sportsnet and Versus. Jones is also my colleague at Sportsradio 610WIP.

Jones has relayed many breathtaking and horrifying stories, but no book would be lengthy enough to contain all of his precious - and interesting - memories. When I inquired about some post-season memories, however, he offered this gem referring to Game 6 of the 1999 Eastern Conference Quarter Finals against the Toronto Maple Leafs:

"I'm sorry this isn't a positive memory, but this one has stuck with me for a while. We were trailing the Leafs three games to two in a hard fought series. We were locked up in a scoreless defensive battle trying to force a Game 7 and with about 3 minutes left, referee Terry Gregson makes a horseshit elbowing call on John LeClair."

The Leafs Sergei Berezen ending up scoring on the power play, giving the Leafs the 1-0 win. They won the series too, but the events that unfolded during post-game were perhaps more memorable than the outcome. Ed Snider was irate with regards to the officiating; what followed was one of the team owner's most impassioned rants on the topic.

"Snider went absolutely nuts. As I'm walking down the tunnel after the game, Mr. Snider grabs me near the locker room and tells me to say whatever the hell I want because he's picking up the fines!"

Snider went on to blast Gregson at length for making a call which should have been under the Rule Book C philosophy when considering the time and place of the infraction.

"I got fined like a thousand dollars for verbal abuse or something like that, poor Mr. Snider got fined like 50G!"

 **Memories from Those Who Wore the Orange and Black**

*Did you know that Eric Lindros holds the team record for most assists in a single regular season game with 6 when he accomplished that feat versus the Ottawa Senators in 1997?*

# FLYER'D UP!

Trivia, Facts, and Anecdotes for Fans of the Orange and Black.

### Bill Clement (1971-1975)

The Flyers selected Bill Clement in the second round of the 1970 NHL Entry Draft. He ended up playing four seasons with the Flyers. Clement was a member of both Stanley Cup winning teams; he scored the second goal in Game 6 of the 1975 Stanley Cup Final against Buffalo to salt the game and the series for the Flyers. Most Flyer fans know him as a passionate professional and an extremely talented hockey broadcaster.

Clement has run the gamut in the broadcasting world, working the color commentary on many hockey games since his retirement. He has provided brilliant and exact analysis for almost every network that covers the NHL. Recently, he has made his way back to the Flyers' family in the broadcast booth and shared some fond memories of his career in Philadelphia.

"That Buffalo series in '75 really sticks out in my mind -- and not because of the goal or any individual stuff, but [because of] the togetherness of our team back then."

Clement was referring to a close-knit group that played for a common goal and left the need for individual success at the door in search of the Stanley Cup.

"The first victory in '74 versus Boston was legendary and I have vivid memories of that series; but, what I will always remember is the plane ride home from Buffalo with our second Stanley Cup. It was just us away from the world, if only for two hours, rejoicing and being together, reflecting on

# FLYER'D UP!

Trivia, Facts, and Anecdotes for Fans of the Orange and Black.

all that we had gone through. It was very intense and very special."

Clement did share this funny memory of the '74 Final versus Boston:

It was Game 6 and time was winding down. The Flyers were ahead 1-0 and the Spectrum was rocking. Clement was about to take a defensive draw in the Flyers zone when he catches goaltender Bernie Parent waving his hands in the air and asking referee Art Skov for time.

"At this point, I'm thinking Bernie is going to offer some sage advice or some interesting information. But no, I lean down so I can hear Bernie through his mask."

Bill Clement: "Yeah Bernie?"
Bernie Parent: " How's it going Bill?"
Bill Clement: "Pretty good, how are you?"
Bernie Parent: "Ok, just checking."

"I won the draw, and we won the cup. That was just Bernie's way of calming everybody down -- and himself, for that matter. Moments of levity were Bernie's best."

### Tim Kerr (1980-1991)
Tim Kerr was a goal-scoring machine for the Flyers. He was regarded as having the best combination of skill and strength as any player of his time. Kerr, who battled countless injuries during his career with the Flyers, had a hulking frame that made him

*The Flyers hulking Tim Kerr creating space against Pittsburgh*

# FLYER'D UP!

Trivia, Facts, and Anecdotes for Fans of the Orange and Black.

an immovable force in front of the opposition's net. His stature helped him set an NHL record for power play goals in a season with 34 in the 1985-86 campaign.

Kerr's scoring prowess allowed him to register four straight 50-plus-goal seasons, as he became the cornerstone of the successful mid-eighties Flyers teams.

Kerr recalls his greatest post-season memory: a game played at Madison Square Garden in the Patrick Division Semi-Finals in April of 1985. It certainly was an incredible match.

Kerr notched four goals in the second period against New York Rangers' goaltender Glen Hanlon; three of the goals came on the power play in just 8 minutes and 16 seconds of action. The Flyers went on to win the game 6-5 and win the series in a three game sweep. Kerr looks back on those terrific hockey teams of the 80's as containing some of the finest moments during his NHL career.

*The first captain in team history Lou Angotti with Leon Rochefort*

"My best accomplishments were being part of some great teams in the 1980's. I miss being around a bunch of teammates that had the same goal of winning."

### Lou Angotti (1967-68)
Lou Angotti does not have a storied past, but was the first player to captain the Philadelphia Flyers. Angotti recorded 12 goals and 37 assists in 70 games with the Flyers, but

*Did you know that Ron Flockhart holds the Flyers record for the fastest two goals by a Flyers player when he scored two goals versus the St. Louis Blues in 1981 in 8 seconds?*

# FLYER'D UP!

Trivia, Facts, and Anecdotes for Fans of the Orange and Black.

was held pointless during the team's first ever playoff series: a defeat in seven games at the hands of the St. Louis Blues.

"My one year was special. Just being a part of the very first Flyers team, an expansion team, and having the success that we did. What a great bunch of guys."

### Simon Nolet (1967-1974)
In 1967, the Flyers filled their brand-new roster with many French Canadian players, many of whom came from the American Hockey League's Quebec Aces which were purchased by the Flyers. Along with Serge Bernier and Leon Rochcfort came Simon Nolet to the orange and black. Like many, Nolet's heart has never left.

On the ice, Nolet was a member of the 1974 Stanley Cup Champions and today he remains a scout for the team in a position he has held since 1990. Nolet states that participating in the NHL was a great accomplishment, but winning Lord Stanley's silver chalice is the ultimate achievement.

"Whcn you win the Cup, you're the best in the world. It's every player's dream, from juniors, to the minor leagues, to the NHL, and mine came true when I played for the Flyers and will always be remembered as a winner."

### Bobby "The Chief" Taylor (1971-1976)
Bobby Taylor made his mark in Philadelphia as the long-time television color analyst and sidekick of Gene Hart. Though Taylor was relegated to back-up goaltending duties for most of his time with the Flyers, he stayed

# FLYER'D UP!

Trivia, Facts, and Anecdotes for Fans of the Orange and Black.

sharp and focused if anything were ever to happen to Bernie Parent. Taylor only appeared in 46 games in the NHL; however, today he is an all-time fan favorite for the Flyers faithful; his great disposition and commitment to teamwork contribute to his popularity. Taylor is also quite the story-teller.

Though Taylor never played in the post-season during the Flyers' playoff runs in the seventies, he looks back on the Cup years with fantastic memories of teamwork, dedication and pride.

"The first Cup was incredible. We beat a pretty amazing team in the Boston Bruins. They had guys like Bobby Orr, Wayne Cashman and Phil Esposito. But then, winning a second time and proving it was no fluke was the best."

Taylor was also popular in the locker room and was a respected teammate. He grew close to the team's captain and leader Bob Clarke, who used that closeness to his advantage.

"I'll never forget the '75 series against Buffalo. We had just lost two straight at The Aud and the Sabres had tied the series at two games apiece. We weren't worried though, because we always had handled Buffalo, especially at home where we were headed for Game 5."

Taylor had realized that even though the team felt confident, Clarke didn't sense urgency and intensity from the collective. While the team was loading

# FLYER'D UP!

Trivia, Facts, and Anecdotes for Fans of the Orange and Black.

the bus for the airport, Taylor was seated at the rear, talking and looking too content. Clarke let him have it.

"'Clarkie' was staring at me like Superman with his vision. He went off on me, explaining that this was the Stanley Cup Finals and that we needed to play better. It was a legendary rant. I knew what he was doing. He did what all great leaders do, he fired up the team."

It must have worked, the Flyers won the next two games and secured their second straight Stanley Cup.

Taylor may not have made a single save on the ice, but was tremendously important off of it.

"Being a team player means putting the team first. Individual accomplishments are nice and make the team look better, but in the end, it's the team and its togetherness that is most important element of winning."

*The Flyers Brad McCrimmen battling the Edmonten Oilers*

***Brad "The Beast" McCrimmon (1982-1987)*** Brad McCrimmon and Mark Howe were arguably the best pair of shutdown defensemen in Flyers' history. They spent five wonderful seasons together, during which time all hockey fans could do was watch in awe.

"[Howe and I] had a special synergy. We'd see the same things; we knew what we were doing out there together. And I'm proud to say that we were great friends and teammates then and we're still the best of bud-

# FLYER'D UP!

Trivia, Facts, and Anecdotes for Fans of the Orange and Black.

dies today."

Like Howe, McCrimmon recalls Game 6 of the 1987 Stanley Cup Finals as his favorite memory as a Flyer.

"I remember in warm-ups, the Spectrum was jam-packed. The place was crazy. It was so loud, that it went quiet -- if that makes any sense. I never heard anything like that in my life, and still haven't."

McCrimmon said playing in the Spectrum was the ultimate experience.

"It was the best building I ever got to play in, the place was rocking every night."

Although McCrimmon tasted the sweet success of winning the Cup in Calgary in 1989, he still recalls the outstanding effort that was made during the team's phenomenal playoff run in 1987.

"Losing that final series to Edmonton in seven games was disappointing, but we gave it all we had. There wasn't an ounce of energy left; the ultimate effort was made and the tank was empty. We held our heads high, though."

### Ron Sutter (1982-91)
When Ron Sutter entered the NHL, he wasn't the only one in his family who would accomplish the feat. Six men from the Sutter family made it to the professional league, including Ron's twin brother Rich, who would also play for the Flyers between 1983 and 1986. Those were the three

# FLYER'D UP!

Trivia, Facts, and Anecdotes for Fans of the Orange and Black.

best seasons of Ron's career.

Sutter was a working-man's player; he was always the first to the rink and willing to do the dirty work. He was at his best in corner battles and, as one of the game's best defensive forwards, he always drew the opposition's best.

The Sutter family and hockey have always intertwined within different towns and franchises, so when Sutter described the Flyers' organization as a "family", the description fit.

"Playing nine seasons with the Flyers was a special accomplishment. Those years we spent knocking on the door of the Stanley Cup were special for me. My time with the Flyers helped me foster a work ethic that forced me to sacrifice my personal goals for the good of the team."

Sutter made an honest effort. His defensive-minded approach on the ice came from the countless hours he spent in the practice rink, a work ethic that he tries to instill in his nine year-old son Riley.

"You have to go to work each day with a purpose, do your best, make yourself better and have a sense of achievement every day. That's what I did with the Flyers and that's what I still do today."

Oftentimes, guys behind the scenes make the wheel spin.

"The unsung heroes are the guys on the third and fourth lines that buy into the system and the top-end talented guys always show their appreciation for the guys who have less talent because they knew it's those players that put them into a position to win."

# FLYER'D UP!

Trivia, Facts, and Anecdotes for Fans of the Orange and Black.

And even though Ron is now a member of the Calgary Flames organization, there's always a place for the Flyers.

"The organization meant a lot to me. My son Riley still cheers for the Flyers because he knows his Dad still holds a soft spot for the orange and the black."

*The Flyers Brad Marsh taking care of Detroit's Ron Duguay*

### Brad Marsh (1981-88)

Brad Marsh was a tough, no-frills defenseman for the Flyers who was always reliable. The Flyers acquired Marsh from the Calgary Flames in exchange for the popular Mel Bridgman in 1981 in what appeared to be an odd trade.

Marsh was one of the last players in the NHL to play without a helmet. While watching Marsh play, one would think with his combative style, he would want all the padding he could get his hands on.

Marsh was a superb shot-blocker and a physical presence in front of the net that knew how to throw his body around. As a respected teammate, he is remembered as a player who epitomized the Flyers' tough style of play.

Like many of his teammates from the eighties, Marsh looks back on the incredible playoff runs with great pride for the efforts, but extreme disappointment for the outcomes.

# FLYER'D UP!

Trivia, Facts, and Anecdotes for Fans of the Orange and Black.

"My time with the Flyers was quite different from a team aspect. I played with five different organizations and I must tell you, other teams just didn't seem to have the same bond."

Marsh recalls that the Flyers' team unity was rare; the bond never showed more than in the spring of 1987 under the guidance of head coach Mike Keenan.

"We did crazy stuff. During the post-season in New York, Keenan took us to see Hoosiers as a team bonding experiment and then I think it was a Broadway play like Dreamgirls or something. Just think of that picture: [25 guys] going to a play in New York City. We drank them out of beer; we were so bored."

No conversation with a player from the 1987 roster can be complete without bringing up Game 7 in Edmonton. Marsh tells his story from a different perspective -- a perspective that reinforces what team unity and togetherness is all about.

"On the plane ride back from Edmonton after Game 7, the plane ran out of booze and beer, so we all got into the red wine. Well, needless to say, you know what red wine does to your teeth and lips? We got off that plane amongst the thousands of fans and as we're being interviewed, almost every single one of us has purple teeth and lips. It was hysterical!"

Marsh realized that evening that his teammates really didn't want the season to end.

"We wanted to keep the party going so we stopped in Jersey along the White Horse Pike at the Evergreen Lounge. There we were, teammates -- even

*Did you know that the Flyers first ever playoff series win came over the Minnesota North Stars when they defeated them 4 games to 2 in the 1972-73 quarterfinals?*

# FLYER'D UP!

Trivia, Facts, and Anecdotes for Fans of the Orange and Black.

Clarkie and Keenan showed up. Our wives, girlfriends and families [were] just celebrating such a tremendous effort. We even got musicians to come in and play for us at seven in the morning. We stayed there for hours, ordered pizzas and then mingled with the regulars all day long."

The team believed that they were going to win Game 7 on Sunday night, but scheduling problems in Edmonton forced the game to be played a day later.

"That extra day off between Game 6 and 7 hurt us. We were in their heads; if the circus didn't come to town, things could have been different."

Twenty-one years later, the pain is still there, but so too are the fantastic memories and friendships.

### *Danny Briere (2007-present)*
Danny Briere has only been a Flyer for a short time, but already feels a part of the organization. Briere was among the most coveted free agents following the 2006/2007 season - presumably, he could have signed anywhere. Briere had just ended a very good season as a member of the Buffalo Sabres; he had come within one game of reaching the Stanley Cup Finals.

Briere had a close friendship with Flyers goaltender Marty Biron, who was traded to the Flyers in February of 2007. The two spent several seasons together as teammates in Buffalo; it is often mentioned that it was because of their friendship that Briere decided to sign to an eight-year, 52 million dollar deal that would likely keep him in a Flyers uniform for the rest of his career.

# FLYER'D UP!

Trivia, Facts, and Anecdotes for Fans of the Orange and Black.

With Briere in tow, the Flyers embarked on a journey to within three games of the Stanley Cup Finals; in doing so, they had completed an incredible turnaround from the previous season which found the organization suffering through their worst year in franchise history.

Briere knew this was the place he was meant to be.

"I'm convinced; I never had a doubt in my mind -- there was just something about the Flyers. Having a chance to play with Simon Gagne, to be reunited with some of my friends and the passion of the Flyer fans, I definitely made the right decision."

During the Flyers' unexpected playoff run in the spring of 2008, Briere recorded nine goals and seven assists. He said that while the entire run was dramatic, he'll never forget the Flyers' Game 7 overtime victory in Washington to defeat the Capitals and send the Philadelphia team to a date with the Montreal Canadiens, a team he spurned as a free agent.

"The excitement of playing in and winning that Game 7 in Washington was unbelievable. You dream of playing in those types of games as a kid. It was unreal. And then when we clinched Game 5 in Montreal, while I was being booed every moment I stepped on the ice, it was just something so special for me about that whole run we had."

### Marty Biron (2007-present)
Biron spent parts of eight seasons with the Sabres. He was traded to Flyers in exchange for a second round draft pick as part of General Manager Paul Holmgren's "reclamation project". Biron quickly started to answer critics' questions as to whether he could be a number one goaltender in the NHL.

 Memories from Those Who Were the Orange and Black

# FLYER'D UP!

Trivia, Facts, and Anecdotes for Fans of the Orange and Black.

Biron's goaltending was the backbone of the Flyers 2008 playoff run, during which time he posted a brilliant performance in the second round versus Montreal. For a boy born in the Canadian province of Quebec, playing against Montreal in the playoffs as a member of the Flyers created fantastic, lasting memories. Biron, Danny Briere, and Simon Gagne each remember walking the Canadian streets of Montreal and having a good time with the fans there.

"Before the games in Montreal, Danny [Briere] and I and Simon [Gagne] would walk down the street and we'd go get some coffee before meeting the rest of the guys for a team dinner.

"And the people in Montreal down on Saint Catherine Street knew, of course, that were French Canadian; they would wish us luck -- but not too much, because we were now the enemy, playing for the Flyers.

"So we get into this coffee shop and, as we were leaving, everybody was booing us and shouting "Let's Go Habs!" and everyone in the place started laughing, and we had such a good time."

Biron felt proud to be a member of the Flyers' organization when the Flyers clinched on Bell Centre ice.

The Flyers beat the first-seeded Canadiens in five games and were on their way to the Eastern Conference Finals.

"Those fans weren't doing it to be nasty. [Briere, Gagne and I] got a kick out of how much fun we were having with them. It was extremely special to win [in Montreal] and clinch on their ice."

Biron hopes there are many more memories to be made in Philadelphia.

"The memories of that playoff run [of 2008] will be something I'll be talking about years from now when I'm sitting down, having a beer, and looking back. The Philadelphia fans meeting and greeting us at the train station, the great playoff run with my teammates -- [it] was just awesome."

### Paul Holmgren (1975-1984)
Paul Holmgren played his first game with the Flyers in 1975. His style of play immediately identified with the fans and made him one of the most popular Flyers in team history. Holmgren has done it all for the orange and black -- played, scouted and coached. He now serves as the team's General Manager.

"Homer" was so special because he was able to combine ferocious play with solid offensive contribution. Holmgren was reliable as a tough-nosed player who was willing to stick up for his teammates. (After all, he did rack up 1,600 penalty minutes throughout his career.) He continued to embody the Flyers combative style of play even as the team drifted away from the "Broad Street Bullies" style; what truly ingratiated Holmgren to hockey fans, however, was that he was a rare heavyweight with a scoring touch.

Holmgren was an integral part of the great 1979-80 Flyers who continue to own the longest unbeaten streak in professional sports history when they went 35 consecutive games without a loss; in fact, Holmgren registered a

*Did you know that Rick MacLeish still holds the team record for most playoff game winning goals with 10? The closest current Flyer on the list is Simon Gagne, with 3.*

# FLYER'D UP!

Trivia, Facts, and Anecdotes for Fans of the Orange and Black.

career-high 30 goals and 65 points during the that season and recalls being part of that team as a highlight of his career.

"Well, for a team accomplishment, the 35-game unbeaten streak was a really cool thing to go through with my teammates. They were a great group of guys with one goal in mind. We were a close knit group."

The streak halted on January 6th, 1980 in a 7-1 loss to the Minnesota North Stars. The Flyers continued their stellar season though, and reached the Stanley Cup Finals versus the New York Islanders. During Game 2 of the series against the Islanders, Holmgren became the first United States-born player to record a hat trick in a Stanley Cup Finals game. Holmgren would have gladly traded that feat and the streak for the Stanley Cup.

"We also played in the Cup Finals that year and on the flip side, we had the agony of defeat in losing. You work all year long to win the Stanley Cup and that's your goal as a player and when you come up short, it's agonizing."

"Homer" hopes to be able to lift Lord Stanley's silver chalice as he continues to mold the Flyers into one of league's elite teams.

### Bob Clarke (1969-1984)
Clarke is the face of the Philadelphia Flyers' franchise. He was the best player to ever wear the orange and black. Clarke spent 15 seasons with the Flyers during which time he recorded 358 goals and 852 assists for 1,210 points. He is a member of both the Flyers' Hall of Fame as well as the Hall of Fame of the NHL. His work ethic, desire, leadership and hockey skills were a template for all Flyers to follow; Clarke was a player that truly led by example. He was the NHL's Most Valuable Player three times and the only captain in Flyers history to hoist the Stanley Cup. His number, 16, will hang

# FLYER'D UP!

Trivia, Facts, and Anecdotes for Fans of the Orange and Black.

forever in the rafters of the Wachovia Center.

Clarke has given most of his adult life to the Flyers organization. While he won the Stanley Cup twice as a player, he also had successful runs as the team's General Manager, leading the team to the Stanley Cup Finals three times. During Clarke's 19 seasons as the GM, the Flyers were at the precipice of victory, but never able to win the Cup. He now serves as Senior Vice President.

Clarke will always be remembered as a Flyer and hockey great and a successful General Manager; however, he is not without criticism. His ill-timed trades and failed personnel decisions will be up for perpetual discussion. Clarke's public feud with Eric Lindros and Lindros' parents was a public relations disaster for the Flyers and will always be part of Clarke's legacy.

However, for Clarke, winning was the only thing he wanted for the Flyers' organization.

"Winning the Stanley Cup is the greatest team accomplishment that any player can have. Individual awards, the MVPs and the Selke award that I won were nice for personal accomplishments, but winning as a team is everything."

Clarke was the leader of the "Broad Street Bullies". It was during the early years of the organization that the Flyers fostered the tradition of family, togetherness and pride. This tradition, Clarke knows, will carry on within the team forever.

"The best stories always involved Bob Kelly. [Kelly and I] lived beside each other for years and we had a lot of fun. That's what I miss the most:

 **Memories from Those Who Were the Orange and Black**

*Did you know that Illka Sinsalo scored his first*
*ever goal in the NHL on a penalty shot?*

# FLYER'D UP!

Trivia, Facts, and Anecdotes for Fans of the Orange and Black.

the times spent as a team; the togetherness as a team."

Clarke's legacy is vast, but ultimately, he wants to be remembered for what was most important.

"The best thing that they can say about me when I die is that I was a good team player and a good friend. That's all you can ask."

*The legendary Bobby Clarke posing with the Stanley Cup*

# FLYER'D UP!

## BEFORE OR AFTER THEY WERE FLYERS

See if you can remember on which teams these Flyers played when they weren't in orange and black.

1. Defenseman Brad McCrimmon played for the Flyers between 1982 and 1987. Before he was a Flyer, he played for:
A) Boston Bruins          C) Chicago Blackhawks
B) Calgary Flames         D) Hartford Whalers

2. Bill Root ended his NHL career with the Flyers, playing in 24 games with the team during the 1987-88 season. For which of the following did he NOT play prior to his joining the Flyers?
A) St. Louis Blues        C) Toronto Maple Leafs
B) Montreal Canadiens     D) Boston Bruins

3. Goaltender Phil Myre played with the Flyers from 1979 until 1981. With which team did he end his career in 1983?
A) Boston Bruins          C) Buffalo Sabres
B) Colorado Rockies       D) Calgary Flames

4. Right-winger Mark Recchi was one of several Flyers to enjoy two different stints with the Flyers. He was a member of all of the following organizations except:
A) Pittsburgh Penguins    C) Boston Bruins
B) Montreal Canadiens     D) Atlanta Thrashers

5. Center Eric Lindros was drafted by the Quebec Nordiques, but played his first game as a Philadelphia Flyer. For which team did he play his last?
A) New York Rangers       C) Toronto Maple Leafs
B) Dallas Stars           D) Minnesota Wild

6. Bob Kelly began his career with the Flyers in 1970. He retired in 1982 as a member of which organization?
A) Pittsburgh Penguins    C) Buffalo Sabres
B) Los Angeles Kings      D) Washington Capitals

7. Goaltender Pete Peeters began and ended his career with the Flyers. Which two teams did he play with in between?
A) Boston Bruins & Washington Capitals          C) Boston Bruins & Winnipeg Jets
B) Washington Capitals & Montreal Canadiens     D) None of the above

86

answers on page 179

# FLYER'D UP!

Trivia, Facts, and Anecdotes for Fans of the Orange and Black.

## BEFORE OR AFTER THEY WERE FLYERS

8. At the end of the 2008 season, center Mike Sillinger had played for 12 different teams, including the Flyers. Which team did he play with the season before coming to the Flyers in 1998?
A) Vancouver Canucks
B) St. Louis Blues
C) New York Islanders
D) Tampa Bay Lightning

9. Jim Montgomery is credited with giving the "Legion of Doom" its nickname. With which team did he end his career?
A) Dallas Stars
B) New Jersey Devils
C) Detroit Red Wings
D) San Jose Sharks

10. Left-winger Jan Hlavac was acquired by the Flyers from the New York Rangers as part of the Eric Lindros deal. The Flyers then traded him a season later to which organization?
A) New York Rangers
B) Carolina Hurricanes
C) Vancouver Canucks
D) Chicago Blackhawks

11. All of the following players played with both the New York Islanders and the Philadelphia Flyers except?
A) Ruslan Fedotenko
B) Trent Klatt
C) Jean Potvin
D) Mike York

12. As of 2008, Mel Bridgman remains the only player the Flyers selected number one overall in the NHL Draft. He played in 977 regular season games for all of the following teams except?
A) New Jersey Devils
B) Atlanta Flames
C) Detroit Red Wings
D) Vancouver Canucks

13. Defenseman Ted Harris finished his career as a member of the 1975 Stanley Cup Champion Philadelphia Flyers. With which team did he begin his playing career?
A) Toronto Maple Leafs
B) Chicago Blackhawks
C) Boston Bruins
D) Montreal Canadiens

14. Current Flyers General Manager Paul Holmgren was drafted by the Flyers and spent parts of nine seasons with the Flyers. He retired a member of the:
A) Pittsburgh Penguins
B) Hartford Whalers
C) Vancouver Canucks
D) Minnesota North Stars

87

**answers on page 179**

# FLYER'D UP!

## BEFORE OR AFTER THEY WERE FLYERS

15.Left wing Ross Lonsberry played for the Flyers from 1971-78 and finished his career as a member of the Pittsburgh Penguins. With which two teams did he play for before becoming a member of the Flyers?
A) Boston Bruins & Los Angeles Kings        C) Boston Bruins & Detroit Redwings
B) Los Angeles Kings & New York Rangers     D) Chicago Blackhawks & Pittsburgh Penguins

16.Center Tim Young finished his NHL career after playing 20 games for the Flyers in 1984-85. Previously, he had played eight seasons as a member of the Minnesota North Stars and one season as a member of the:
A) Edmonton Oilers          C) Winnipeg Jets
B) Quebec Nordiques         D) Hartford Whalers

17.Left wing Dainius Zubrus played his first two seasons in the NHL with the Flyers. With which team did he play for next (after being traded by the club in 1999)?
A) Washington Capitals      C) Florida Panthers
B) Montreal Canadiens       D) Buffalo Sabres

18.All of the following players played for both the Philadelphia Flyers and the Chicago Blackhawks except:
A) Doug Crossman            C) Garry Galley
B) Alexei Zhamnov           D) Peter White

19.The Flyers signed Joel Otto as a free agent in 1995. Until that season, Otto had played his entire career for which team?
A) St. Louis Blues          C) Calgary Flames
B) Pittsburgh Penguins      D) Toronto Maple Leafs

20.Randy Holt played for which team the season prior to his being signed as a free agent by the Flyers in 1983?
A) Washington Capitals      C) Chicago Blackhawks
B) Los Angeles Kings        D) Calgary Flames

answers on page 179

# FLYER'D UP!

Trivia, Facts, and Anecdotes for Fans of the Orange and Black.

# REMEMBERING GENE HART

*The following is personal account of Lauren Hart, the daughter of the legendary Flyers' broadcaster Gene Hart. Lauren is currently a professional recording artist who sings the National Anthem at the Wachovia Center. Gene was a member of the Flyers family as the team's broadcaster for 29 years, during which time he announced more than 2,000 NHL games. Although Hart passed away in 1999, his voice and memory are alive in the hearts and minds of the Flyer family and its fans.*

I remember finding a tattered black leather autograph book when I was 10 years old. The book had belonged to my father when he was young; written on the first page was his name and underneath it said, "I want to be a hockey announcer". Even then, as he listened to hockey games on the radio in New York City, he knew where his heart was. That love -- the love of hockey -- was never lost.

My father's dream was fulfilled when he received a call in the late 60's to join the Philadelphia Flyers as their broadcaster. He looked at my mom and said, "I'm a star!" Throughout his many years as an announcer, my father taught sports fans in Philadelphia the game of hockey and, as a result, they fell in love with the big guy with the sparkling eyes who was "The Voice".

For fans, my dad's excitement was their excitement and, on the other end, his loss was their loss. My dad connected with the Flyer faithful because of his knowledge. People couldn't believe the way he memorized each and every player, each and every stat, and each and every minute. All that information was kept in a set of black books, which he filled with numbers and facts. His listeners were surprised to know that he learned Russian -- which was how he was able to pronounce all those crazy Russian names when the Red Army arrived in Philly to play the Broad Street Bullies.

# FLYER'D UP!

Trivia, Facts, and Anecdotes for Fans of the Orange and Black.

He had a passion that carried through his voice and into the hearts of Flyer fans. He loved it. Fans could feel it.

Growing up, he was always just "Dad". He was a regular guy like all the other dads in the neighborhood. I knew what he did, but I never really understood how much he was loved until I went to college at Temple University. One afternoon, I called for a ride home. There he was, with the big old sedan and license plates that read VOICE; his sunroof was open and his cigar all fired up. I jumped in and, as we drove down the main street, campus kids jumped into the road yelling, "Gene! Geno! Big Gene! Gene Hart -- there he is! That's the voice of the Flyers!" With a huge grin on his face, my dad waved; I never saw anything like it. Who was this man -- my father?

In the same way, I have carried my own passion for music since I was a kid. I never thought my love -- music -- and my father's -- hockey -- would cross as they have in the Hart family. I had always wanted to sing the National Anthem for the team. I watched as other girls sang and waited for my turn. Dad wanted to make sure that I worked for the chance to sing on my own, so he didn't pull any strings. I finally received the opportunity in the Spectrum. Waiting in the tunnel as The Great One walked by to take the ice, I was nervous. I wanted to be just as great as Dad was. I wanted to be the other "voice".

Dad passed away in 1999. Not a day goes by where I don't hear about my father: how much he meant to a fan; how he was just like a father to them; how he helped someone outside of the arena; how he visited someone sick; how he had leant them money. It was amazing to learn so much more about him -- things I never even knew. That year, I was determined to sing at every game in his honor. Little did I know, that season would change my own future. I had cancer.

I asked the team if they wanted me to continue. That year, I made every game except for one. All forces converged that season; fans were mourning Dad's loss and rooting for my recovery.

**Remembering Gene Hart**

The bond between me, my family, and the fans was incredible. In my worst moment, all I could feel was the magic. Thousands of people I never met tirelessly cheered for me every night. All of the great things the fans felt for my dad, I now felt. Philadelphia hockey fans will never know the depths of their importance in my healing.

The season ended up with "God Bless America" and a loss to the New Jersey Devils . The team was only one game away from going to the Cup. I found out then that I was in remission.

I have always felt that in some way my dad has been watching over me from the press box up high in the building. I still look up there every night. If my father were here, I don't think he would believe how the story has unfolded. I think he would be proud.

Somehow music and hockey came together just when I needed it most.
  Dad, you were -- and are -- the best. Thanks.

## Brian's Top 5 Favorite Sayings from Gene Hart:
**5: "There's a mass of humanity in front of the Flyers net."**
**4: "And Bobby, you can see it now, the Flyers have stopped skating."**
**3: "Fasten your seatbelts, my friends -- we're in for a real humdinger!"**
**2: "He shoots, he scores! Bobby Clarke scores for a case of Tastykakes!"**
**1: "Good night; good hockey."**

**And, Gene's most famous line:**
**"Ladies and Gentlemen, the Flyers are going to win the Stanley Cup! The Flyers win the Stanley Cup! The Flyers win the Stanley Cup! The Flyers have won the Stanley Cup!"**

**Thanks for the memories, Gene.**

# FLYER'D UP!

## FLYERS' FIRSTS TRIVIA

1. Who was the Flyers' opponent in their first-ever regular season game?
A. Chicago Blackhawks    B. St. Louis Blues
C. California Seals    D. Boston Bruins

2. Who served as Flyers' first-ever coach?
A. Keith Allen    B. Fred Shero
C. Lou Nanne    D. Al Arbour

3. Who was the Flyers' first opponent at the Spectrum?
A. New York Rangers    B. New York Islanders
C. Pittsburgh Penguins    D. Montreal Canadiens

4. Who scored the first Flyers' goal at the Core States Center?
A. Eric Lindros    B. John Leclair
C. Jiri Latal    D. Dainus Zubrus

5. Who did the Flyers face in their first game at the Core States Center?
A. Colorado Avalanche    B. Tampa Bay Lightning
C. New York Islanders    D. Florida Panthers

6. Who led the Flyers in goals scored in their first season?
A. Leon Rochefort    B. Lou Angotti
C. Lew Morrison    D. Bobby Clarke

7. Who led the Flyers in assists during their first season?
A. Lou Angotti    B. Leon Rochefort
C. Larry Zeidel    D. Forbes Kennedy

8. Which player led the Flyers in penalty minutes during their first season?
A. Ed Van Impe    B. Larry Zeidel
C. Bob Currier    D. Brit Selby

9. Dave Poulin wore #20 for the Flyers for most of his career. Which number did he wear first?
A. 21    B. 39    C. 34    D. 40

92

**answers on page 179**

# FLYER'D UP!

Trivia, Facts, and Anecdotes for Fans of the Orange and Black.

## FLYERS' FIRSTS TRIVIA

10. Which team did the Flyers face in their first playoff series?
A. Chicago Blackhawks    B. Minnesota North Stars
C. New York Islanders    D. St. Louis Blues

11. Which team did the Flyers defeat for their first playoff series win?
A. Chicago Blackhawks    B. Minnesota North Stars
C. New York Islanders    D. St. Louis Blues

12. Which was the first team from Canada that the Flyers defeated in a playoff series?
A. Toronto Maple Leafs    B.Montreal Canadiens
C. Vancouver Canucks    D. Edmonton Oilers

13. Which was the first season the Flyers missed the playoffs?
A. 1967-68        B. 1968-69        C. 1969-70        D. 1971-72

14. Which right-winger has scored the most playoff goals in Flyers' history?
A. Reggie Leach        B. Tim Kerr
C. Rick Tocchet        D. Mark Recchi

15. Who was the first Flyer to attempt a penalty shot during a regular season game?
A. Orest Kindrachuk        B. Bill Clement
C. Bill Barber        D. Rick MacLeish

16. Who was the first Flyer to score a goal on a penalty shot during a regular season game?
A. Orest Kindrachuk        B. Bill Clement
C. Bill Barber        D. Rick MacLeish

17. Who was the first Flyers' goaltender to stop a penalty shot by an opponent?
A. Doug Favell        B. Bernie Parent
C. Pete Peters        D. Pelle Lindbergh

18. Who was the first Flyer to record a hat trick?
A. Rosarie Paiment        B. Bobby Clarke
C. Leon Rochefort        D. Gary Dornhoefer

93

**answers on page 179**

# FLYER'D UP!

Trivia, Facts, and Anecdotes for Fans of the Orange and Black.

## FLYERS' FIRSTS

19. Against which team did the Flyers record their first regular season overtime victory?
A. Calgary Flames      B. Pittsburgh Penguins
C. Winnipeg Jets       D. New York Rangers

20. Who was the first Flyer to score an overtime goal in the playoffs?
A. Bobby Clarke        B. Leon Rochefort
C. Don Blackburn       D. Dave Schultz

21. Who was the first-ever Flyers' draft pick?
A. Bob Currier         B. Serge Bernier
C. Al Sarault          D. Lew Morrison

22. Who was the only player to be selected first overall in the NHL draft by the Flyers?
A. Peter Forsberg      B. Eric Lindros
C. Mel Bridgman        D. Mike Ricci

23. Who was the first player to wear number 7?
A. Lou Angotti         B. Bill Barber
C. Al Sarault          D. Reggie Fleming

24. Who is the first Flyer to have his last name begin with the letter "O"?
A. Joel Otto           B. Adam Oates
C. Randy Osburn        D. Gino Odjick

25. Who was the Flyers' first general manager?
A. Keith Allen         B. Bud Polie
C. Al Arbour           D. Ed Snider

26. All of the following players selected in the 2003 NHL draft have played at least one game for the Flyers except:
A) Alexandre Picard    B) Ryan Potulny
C) Colin Fraser        D) Stefan Ruzicka

94

**answers on page 179**

# FLYER'D UP!

Trivia, Facts, and Anecdotes for Fans of the Orange and Black.

## NHL TEAMS WORD SEARCH

```
C L R G R F M T G O F H Y X A T
D H Y N E T I O I S G S C I W L
N Y I S L A N D E R S R O N A F
A C P C W R N E U U N E L E T T
S C O E A A E B W A I G U O T N
H A N L T G S V O J A N M H O E
V L T O O T O H U N E A B P A T
I G N L T R T T I O O R U A M E
L A I I A N A L N N C Y S O A S
L R P U M N O D C O G N N E T O
E Y A A P R T M O A R T A I Y J
B U F F A L O A D J R O O V O N
M R H C B S U O A E R R T N T A
M I E H A N A Y A S T L O U I S
O O F N Y O R L O E B O S T O N
L E L F L O R I D A S A L L A D
```

| | | | |
|---|---|---|---|
| ANAHEIM | ATLANTA | BOSTON | BUFFALO |
| CALGARY | CAROLINA | CHICAGO | COLORADO |
| COLUMBUS | DALLAS | DETROIT | EDMONTON |
| FLORIDA | LA | MINNESOTA | MONTREAL |
| NASHVILLE | NEWJERSEY | NYISLANDERS | NYRANGERS |
| OTTAWA | PHOENIX | PITTSBURGH | STLOUIS |
| SANJOSE | TAMPABAY | TORONTO | VANCOUVER |
| WASHINGTON | | | |

95

**answers on page 182**

# FLYER'D UP!

Trivia, Facts, and Anecdotes for Fans of the Orange and Black.

# FLYERS' ALL-AMERICAN, ALL-EUROPEAN AND ALL-FRENCH CANADIAN TEAMS

*(one season minimum)*

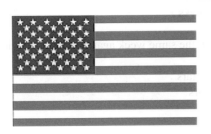

**All-American:**
G: John Vanbiesbrouck
D: Mark Howe
D: Eric Weinrich
LW: John LeClair
C: Joel Otto
RW: Paul Holmgren

**All-European:**
G: Pelle Lindbergh
D: Kimmo Timonen
D: Kim Johnsson
LW: Ilkka Sinisalo
C: Peter Forsberg
RW: Mikael Renberg

**All-French Canadian:**
G: Bernie Parent
D: Moose Dupont
D: Eric Desjardins
LW: Simon Gagne
C: Daniel Briere
RW: Simon Nolet

# FLYER'D UP!

## HAT TRICKS TRIVIA

1. Which player recorded the first hat trick in Flyers history?
A. Leon Rochefort       B. Andre Lacroix
C. Gary Dornhoefer      D. Simon Nolet

2. Against which team did Rick MacLeish record his first hat trick as a Flyer?
A. Montreal Canadiens   B. New York Islanders
C. Boston Bruins        D. Chicago Blackhawks

3. In 1974, Dave Shultz recorded 2 hat tricks in the same week against which opponents?
A. New York Rangers and New York Islanders
B. Chicago Blackhawks and Minnesota North Stars
C. New York Rangers and Minnesota North Stars
D. St. Louis Blues and New York Rangers

4. Against which team did Bob Clarke record his first-ever hat trick?
A. New York Islanders   B. Montreal Canadiens
C. Toronto Maple Leafs  D. Boston Bruins

5. Who were the first two Flyers to record hat tricks in the same game?
A. Bob Clarke and Rick MacLeish       B. Bob Clarke and Ross Lonsberry
C. Bob Clarke and Simon Nolet         D. Ross Lonsberry and Rick MacLeish

6. Which player recorded the first 4 goal game in Flyer history?
A. Bob Clarke           B. Leon Rochefort
C. Rick MacLeish        D. Bill Flett

7. All of these players have had four-goal games as Flyers EXCEPT:
A. Tim Kerr             B. Eric Lindros
C. Bill Barber          D. Bob Clarke

8. Who was the first player to record a hat trick for the Flyers in 1980?
A. Bill Barber          B. Brian Propp
C. Paul Holmgren        D. Mel Bridgman

98

answers on page 179

# FLYER'D UP!

Trivia, Facts, and Anecdotes for Fans of the Orange and Black.

## HAT TRICKS TRIVIA

9. Who recorded the first natural hat trick in team history?
A. Bill Barber          B. Bill Flett
C. Bob Clarke           D. Gary Dornhoefer

10. Who was the first Flyer to record a hat trick in a playoff game?
A. Leon Rochefort       B. Claude Laforge
C. Rosaire Paiement     D. Bill Barber

11. On December 11, 1977, Flyers defenseman Tom Bladon recorded an eight point game with four goals and four assists. Against which team did he accomplish this feat?
A. Minnesota North Stars        B. Kansas City Scouts
C. Washington Capitals          D. Cleveland Barons

12. The Flyers scored a franchise-high 13 goals against the Vancouver Canucks on October 18, 1984. Two players recorded hat tricks. Who were they?
A. Brian Propp and Tim Kerr          B. Illka Sinasalo and Dave Poulin
C. Lindsay Carson and Dave Poulin    D. Illka Sinasalo and Brian Propp

13. Who recorded the 100th hat trick in team history?
A. Bob Clarke           B. Tim Kerr
C. Dave Poulin          D. Rick Tocchet

14. Who was the only player in Flyers history to record a four-goal, natural hat trick in the playoffs?
A. Reggie Leach         B. Tim Kerr
C. Eric Lindros         D. John LeClair

15. Against which team did Eric Lindros record his first NHL hat trick?
A. Quebec Nordiques     B. Ottawa Senators
C. Winnipeg Jets        D. Hartford Whalers

16. All of the following players recorded four-goal games in the 90's EXCEPT:
A. Kevin Dineen         B. John LeClair
C. Eric Lindros         D. Mark Recchi

99

**answers on page 179**

# FLYER'D UP!

Trivia, Facts, and Anecdotes for Fans of the Orange and Black.

## HAT TRICKS TRIVIA

17. During which season did the Flyers fail to record a single hat trick?
A. 2006-2007          B. 1969-1970
C. 1971-1972          D. 1980-1981

18. During which season did the Flyers record the most hat tricks as a team?
A. 1986-1987    B. 1984-1985    C. 1987-1988    D. 1974-1975

19. Who was the last Flyers' defenseman to record a hat trick in the playoffs?
A. Mark Howe          B. Eric Desjardins
C. Andy Delmore       D. Petr Svoboda

21. Who is the only Russian player ever to record a hat trick for the Flyers?
A. Viacheslav Butsayev    B. Dmitry Tertyshny
C. Andrei Lomakin         D. Alexi Zhamnov

22. Against which team did Flyers center Mike Richards record his first hat trick?
A. New York Rangers       B. New York Islanders
C. San Jose Sharks        D. Washington Capitals

23. Against which goalie did the Flyers record their first hat trick?
A. Rogie Vachon           B. Glenn Hall
C. Bruce Gamble           D. Gerry Cheevers

24. Who was the first Flyers player to record a hat trick with the third goal scored on an empty net?
A. Bob Clarke             B. Mel Bridgman
C. Rick Tocchet           D. Ray Allison

25. Which Flyer recorded the only hat trick during the 2003-2004 season?
A. Keith Primeau          B. Tony Amonte
C. Simon Gagne            D. John LeClair

**answers on page 179**

# FLYER'D UP!

Trivia, Facts, and Anecdotes for Fans of the Orange and Black.

# FLASHES IN THE PAN:
## A COLLECTION OF FLYERS WHO STARTED
## BETTER THAN THEY FINISHED
*Brian Startare and Bill Meltzer*

*1. Todd Bergen:* The center's NHL career was brief and controversial. He took Mike Keenan's abrasive coaching style very personally, and never really enjoyed hockey much in the first place. He vacillated between seeking a pro golfing career and playing hockey, and cost himself what could have been a fine hockey career without finding success on the links, either.

Bergen made an immediate splash when he was called up from the AHL as an injury recall on January 10, 1985. He scored two goals against the Canucks in his NHL debut, including the game winner, but pulled an abdominal muscle in his next game. Upon his return on March 10, 1985, he had a goal and two assists in an 11-4 romp over the Penguins. By the end of the regular season, he racked up an eye-popping 11 goals in 14 games. In the playoffs, he had 13 points in 17 games as the Flyers drove to the Stanley Cup Finals. His defensive play left something to be desired, but he was still producing offensively.

As a reward for his strong rookie showing, the Flyers signed him to a multi-year dear. But the player, citing a desire to become a PGA golfer and attend college, decided not to report for training camp before the 1985-86 season. He then announced his retirement from hockey. Bergen's eccentric behavior and outspokenness outraged GM Bob Clarke, who suspended him for

*Did you know that Flyers goaltender Doug Favell recorded the team's first shutout in 1967 with a 1-0 blanking of the Pittsburgh Penguins?*

# FLYER'D UP!

Trivia, Facts, and Anecdotes for Fans of the Orange and Black.

the entire season. The player, through his agent, replied that he didn't care because he was done with hockey, anyway.

Bergen never played another NHL game.

***2. Ron Flockhart:*** The Smithers, British Columbia native's wide-open style of "Flocky Hockey" created a brief sensation in Philadelphia during his rookie season (1981-82) when he scored 33 goals.

The bloom quickly fell off the rose, however, as it became apparent that Flockhart was a one-trick pony who absolutely had to score in order to make a positive contribution on the ice. After two-plus seasons with the Flyers, he was traded to the Penguins and became an NHL journeyman, scoring 145 goals in 453 regular season games but appearing in just 19 playoff tilts. Flockhart however still holds the Flyers record for the scoring the fastest two goals when he netted a pair versus the St. Louis Blues in 8 seconds on December 6, 1981.

***3. Robbie Moore:*** The tiny (5-foot-5) goalie signed in 1978 as an undrafted free agent from the University of Michigan was a great Cinderella story during the 1978-79 season. With Hall of Fame goaltender Bernie Parent having been forced to retire in February due to an eye injury, Moore was called up on March 2. After backing up Wayne Stephenson and Rick St. Croix for two games, Moore made his NHL debut on March 6, against the lowly Colorado Rockies and turned back 22 routine shots for a 5-0 shutout win.

He went on to start three more games, shutting out Vancouver in a 5-0 win, beating St. Louis 5-3, and mopping up for Stephenson in the third period of an ugly 9-2 loss to the Islanders. He posted a tidy 1.77 goals against aver-

# FLYER'D UP!

Trivia, Facts, and Anecdotes for Fans of the Orange and Black.

age and .929 save percentage for his five appearances, thanks mostly to the two shutouts.

Moore was given five starts in the playoffs. Unfortunately, the New York Rangers exposed him for what he actually was-- an undersized minor league goaltender who could get picked apart high to the glove side. He was strafed in three of his five games, posting a 4.03 goals against average and an ugly .838 save percentage.

Moore returned to the minor leagues for the remainder of his career, except for a one-game mop-up appearance with the Washington Capitals in 1982-83.

**4. *Al Hill:*** Hill was a no-frills player who had a respectable little Flyers career as a versatile foot soldier, but deserves to be on this list because of his record-setting NHL debut on February 14, 1977. Setting a mark that still stands, Hill tallied five points (two goals, three assists) in his first NHL game, while playing on all four lines and also having a fight. After that brilliant night in 1977 the Flyers were hoping for more than just 38 more goals over the next ten years. they didn't get it.

**5. *Tim Tookey:*** A classic example of a minor league star who was just a little too slow to translate that success to the NHL. Tookey had cups of coffee with the Capitals, Nordiques, Flyers and Bruins, totaling 106 NHL games, but is best known for his 141-point junior season with Portland and his many years as a prolific AHL scorer for the Hershey Bears.

At any rate, Tookey did have a moment in the sun as a member of the Flyers' NHL squad. With the Flyers riddled with injuries during their run to the 1987 Stanley Cup Finals, the team called up Tookey during the playoffs.

# FLYER'D UP!

Trivia, Facts, and Anecdotes for Fans of the Orange and Black.

After the Flyers split the first two games of the Wales Conference Quarter-finals with the New York Islanders, the battered club faced the difficult task of having to go to Long Island for the next two games.

The Flyers won both, thanks in no small part to Tookey setting up Brian Propp for the game winner in Game 3 and contributing a goal and an assist in the next game. Al Hill also scored goals in both games. Tookey was an awesome minor league player and fan favorite in Hershey but had the rare distinction in Flyers history of recording more career playoff goals for the Flyers (1) then he did in the regular season (0).

## *Great Expectations, No Results*

- *Pavel Brendl:* Brendl was drafted fourth overall in the 1999 draft by the New York Rangers as a highly touted junior star but his promise never came to fruition. He came to Flyers in the forced Eric Lindros trade and played just 50 games for the orange and black, recording just 6 goals and 7 assists. The Flyers correctly gave up on him, sending him to Carolina along with Bruno St. Jacques for Sammi Kapanen. He would go on to play just 28 more games in the NHL with Carolina and Phoenix scoring 5 measly goals.

- *Jiri Dopita:* Once regarded as the best player currently not playing in the NHL, the Flyers convinced the one time Czech player of the year to come to the NHL for the 2001-02 season after acquiring his rights from the Florida Panthers. Dopita was a bust, scoring just 11 goals for the Flyers before injuring his knee. To make matters worse, Dopita scored 4 of those 11 on a chilly January night at home in 2002 versus the lowly Atlanta Thrashers. Dopita was shipped off to Edmon-

**Flashes in the Pan**

---

*Did you know that Bobby Clarke scored the team's first ever regular season overtime goal when he scored against the Pittsburgh Penguins on November 20, 1983?*

# FLYER'D UP!

Trivia, Facts, and Anecdotes for Fans of the Orange and Black.

ton where he played in just 21 more games before returning home to his native Czech Republic.

• *Pat Falloon:* Falloon was drafted first overall in the 1991 NHL Entry Draft by the San Jose Sharks, directly ahead of future Flyer Eric Lindros. A can't miss prospect, Falloon registered 59 points his rookie season but never surpassed that total. He was traded to the Flyers in 1995, where the Flyers gave up a prospect, and a first and fourth rounder. Falloon played in 144 games for the Flyers scoring just 38 goals. As a side note, the first rounder the Flyers surrendered, later was moved to Phoenix where the Coyotes selected Danny Briere.

• *Alexandre Daigle:* The bust of all busts. Daigle was another first overall selection, taken by the Ottawa Senators in the 1993 draft. Daigle entered the NHL with high expectations and the largest starting salary in league history. In four and half seasons, Daigle registered just 74 goals and was characterized by many as lazy and lacking true motivation. The Flyers took a chance on him by sending the aforementioned bust Pat Falloon and Vaclav Prospal for his rights, hoping a change of scenery would do him wonders. Daigle played in just 68 games for the Flyers, scoring just 12 goals. After a few more brief stints, Daigle was out of the NHL and was last seen playing in Switzerland.

*Honorable Mention:* Glen Seabrooke, Brian Dobbin, Ryan Sittler*, Mark Suzor, Danny Lucas, Darren Rumble, Maxime Ouellet, Joni Pitkanen

*Never played a single game in the NHL.*

# FLYER'D UP!

## FLYERS PLAYERS NAME SCRAMBLE

Can you figure out who these Flyers players are by rearranging the letters to form their first and last names?

1. YITMRD  VAOAFKNANSE    _____    _____

2. FJEF  HRNUCCYH    _____    _____

3. LONAN  GRTNMAUBREA    _____    _____

4. RRBAY  NDEA    _____    _____

5. RICE  JSSDENIDAR    _____    _____

6. MTHOSA  SSKRIENO    _____    _____

7. NUSRLAN  KENOOTDEF    _____    _____

8. RINTAM  NERGERI    _____    _____

9. NEL  BHACHRNO    _____    _____

10. RAGY  NNISES    _____    _____

11. TPKIRA  LNIJUH    _____    _____

12. REDNAI  NELAVOKOK    _____    _____

13. DLCAUE  FGALREO    _____    _____

14. NNLEG  VEANNLUM    _____    _____

15. CIR  SSTTRENA    _____    _____

106

answers on page 180

# FLYER'D UP!

Trivia, Facts, and Anecdotes for Fans of the Orange and Black.

## FLYERS PLAYERS NAME SCRAMBLE

16. OGNI  JCKIDO

17. MOT  LDOBAN

18. MISNO  ONTEL

19. YRAN  LUTOPYN

20. NDA  NNQIU

21. VADE  GGDURENSU

22. MIT  OOTYKE

23. TTIECOS  LUHSALP

24. MORAN  PTAOV

25. SEW  ZWLA

26. HRISC  NSNWIE

27. TMIDYIR  HUSYHICVEK

28. NASOJ  TEZN

29. LYERAZ  SLAPKIZA

30. HOJN  BSIEKCROUBNAV

**answers on page 180**

# FLYER'D UP!

Trivia, Facts, and Anecdotes for Fans of the Orange and Black.

Trivia, Facts, and Anecdotes for Fans of the Orange and Black.

# PUGILSM 101

### *with long-time Flyer fan Todd Flynn*

The Flyers have had a long and rich history of being one of the toughest teams in the NHL, both for their style of play and their willingness to drop their mitts and take matters into their own hands. Longtime Flyers fan Todd Flynn and I took a trip down memory lane over a few beers and now provide you with some pugilism fodder that ranges from the Broad Street Bullies themselves to the fighters of today. Enjoy.

The Noel Picard sucker punch on Claude LaForge was "the shot heard around the hockey world." Soon after the hit, Ed Snider entered a four decade plus nuclear arms race that has produced a lineage of tough guys. The fighter's heroic legacies ingratiated in the souls of blue-collar Philadelphians everywhere. So many in other inferior cities despise these legends and often suggest that their respective pictures adorn post office walls with the words "Most Wanted" a notch above. Here, in Philly, that couldn't be farther from the truth.

Fred Shero was PT Barnum and into opposing arenas, he brought a circus known as the Broad Street Bullies, consisting of many perceived animals, most notably, a Hound, a Moose, and a Big Bird. It came equipped with a Hammer. But, there was only one problem: no one wanted this circus in town. Women and children hid, grown men trembled in fear. This circus had numerous magic tricks with the grand finale ultimately culminating with pulling two Stanley Cups out of a hat. There were also many amusement rides in this circus, including a rollercoaster of destruction that had

# FLYER'D UP!

Trivia, Facts, and Anecdotes for Fans of the Orange and Black.

run roughshod through other team's barns for over 40 years, creating brawl-filled memories that will live on forever. Seated on that very rollercoaster was a collection of tough guys rivaled by no franchise in the history of the game.

*Two of the best Flyers fighters of all time, Dave Schultz and Jack McIlhargey in a familiar setting*

These tough guys played for the crest on the front, not the name on the back, they handed-out frontier justice, they brought a level of excitement and intimidation never seen before, they formed the culture of a hockey-starved city, and more importantly, they beat the snot out of the opposition

**Pugilsm 101**

*Did you know that goaltender Gary Innes is the only Flyers player to have a last name beginning with the letter I?*

# FLYER'D UP!

Trivia, Facts, and Anecdotes for Fans of the Orange and Black.

on a nightly basis. These tough guys are true warriors, true gladiators, the Spectrum their domain, the rabid fan base all the adrenaline they need to perform their due diligence.

They came in eras and handed down fistic prowess like high-schoolers do varsity letter jackets. Schultz, Kelly, Saleski, and Moose built the foundation and were the original pioneers. Next came Hoyda, Holmrgen, Bridgman, Wilson, and Wolfman Jack who ushered in a new group of young ruffians that consisted of Brownie, Cochrane, Richter, Berube, Tocchet, Carkner, and Chychrun. Then came the Dan Line, a Fridge, and Big Donald. Today, Riley Cote proudly carries the torch.

Many others were sprinkled in along the way including aging enforcers from other teams like Secord, Fotiu, Hospadar, Odjick, McCarthy, and Cronin the Barbarian. Some we would like to wholeheartedly forget like Roman Vopat, Dale Kushner, Claude Boivin, and Shawn Antoski. Some came in multiple tours like Berube, Tocchet, Brownie, and Fridge. Some got away like Jim Cummins and Chris Simon. Some were flat-out crazy like Billy Tibbetts, Jesse Boulerice, and PJ Stock. Some didn't come at all like Frank the Animal and Stone Cold McLaren. I'll let you guys fill in the rest!

### Best All-Time Flyers Knock-outs

1) Scott Mellanby lands a massive right on the button of Quebec's Jeff Jackson and knocks him out cold; this was the hardest punch that we have ever seen landed in a Flyer's fight.
2) Behn Wilson drops Detroit's John Hillworth behind the net and continues to land three more big rights while Hillworth is out cold on the ice.
3) Dave Schultz renders Montreal's John Van Boxmeer useless as he knocks him out at center ice on a nationally televised game.

# FLYER'D UP!

Trivia, Facts, and Anecdotes for Fans of the Orange and Black.

### Favorite Bench Clear

It has to be the Flyers-Canadiens pre-game brawl in the 1987 playoffs, it truly had it all. I still have fond images carved in my memory of a shirtless Dave Brown hammering Chris Nilan, a young Rick Tocchet taking on John Kordic, and Hospadar pounding on a gutless Claude Lemieux. How about Doug Crossman out on the ice in slippers? Hextall was being restrained in the locker room and was not let out on the ice. A very young Pat Croce was out on the ice during the brawl as he was the Flyers trainer at the time and Don Nachbaur ended-up having his nose broken by his boyhood idol, Larry Robinson. Unreal.

### Bad Beatings

A 19-year-old Lindros taking it to Scott Stevens by landing massive upper-cuts at will, Brashear literally cracking Ranger Sandy McCarthy's helmet in half after peppering him with 30 unanswered punches in a preseason game, Dave Brown breaking Ken Baumgartner's orbital bone, Rookie Craig Berube busting open Bob Probert and making a name for himself in one of his first few fights, Dave Schultz abusing Dale Rolfe, Hound Dog Kelly hammering Steve Durbano after Durbano knocked the teeth out of the mouth of the Flyer's trainer with his stick, and Rick Tocchet dropping Calgary's Paul Baxter.

### Greatest Villains

Tie Domi, Terry O'Reilly, Matthew Barnaby, Dale Hunter, Darcy Tucker, The Plager Brothers, Claude Lemieux, Scott Stevens, Ulf Samuelsson, Igor Ulanov, Ed Jovanovski, Rich Pilon, Troy Crowder, Tiger Williams, Stan Johnathan, Clark Gillies, Darius Kasparaitis, just to name a few!

### Changing of the Guard

In Dave Schultz's return game to the Spectrum with the Kings against the Flyers, he proceeded to pick a fight with a youngster by the name of Paul

# FLYER'D UP!

Trivia, Facts, and Anecdotes for Fans of the Orange and Black.

Holmgren, who was wearing a full cage at the time because of an eye injury. At first, Holmgren didn't oblige because of the affliction, but Schultz pressed the issue and Holmgren beat the tar out of him after taking off his cage.

*Dave Hoyda, another Flyers brawler who missed the top 10*

***Top 10 (No Particular Order)***
Behn Wilson
Dave Brown
Mel Bridgman
Paul Holmgren
Dave Schultz
Craig Berube
Jack McIlhargey
Glen Cochrane
Donald Brashear
Rick Tocchet

### *Anyone Remember?*

• The Dave Brown-Daryl Stanley Bruise Brothers Tee shirt?
• The Ray-May-Barnaby line for the Sabres?
• Eric Lindros beating Chris Simon badly in Quebec City during a pre season game?
• Dale Hunter's elbow on Gord Murphy later triggering an all-out brawl?
• Tocchet head-butting Bob Probert during a vicious fight?
• Behn Wilson beating Gillies?
• Bridgman getting the best of Bobby Nystrom?
• Hextall wiping the floor with Alain Chevrier?
• The name Chris Falcone?
• Dave Brown stepping in and tuning up the late John Kordic after John tried to fight his brother Dan?

**Pugilsm 101**

*Did you know that Bob McCammon was the only Flyers coach in their history to coach the team in two different stints with the club? McCammon first coached the club in 1978-79 and was replaced by Pat Quinn but returned to coach the team again for three seasons.*

## NICKNAMES

Can you match these Flyer players with their nicknames?

| | | |
|---|---|---|
| A. Bob Kelly | *Z* | Sammy |
| B. Dave Schultz | *Y* | Roo |
| C. Larry Goodenough | *X* | Gags |
| D. Mark LaForest | | Thundermouth |
| E. Ed Hospodar | *A* | The Hound |
| F. Reggie Leach | *E* | Boxcar |
| G. Eric Lindros | *W* | Cowboy |
| H. Ken Linesman | *P* | Chico |
| I. Chris Therien | *R* | Boosh |
| J. Bobby Taylor | *B* | The Hammer |
| K. John Vanbiesbrouck | *S* | Frosty |
| L. Andre Dupont | *F* | The Rifle |
| M. Don Saleski | *I* | Bundy |
| N. Bob Dailey | *C* | Izzy |
| O. Joe Watson | *H* | The Rat |
| P. Glen Resch | *D* | Trees |
| Q. Eric Desjardins | *G* | The Big E |
| R. Brian Boucher | *Q* | Rico |
| S. Bob Froese | *K* | Beezer |
| T. Miroslav Dvorak | *J* | Chief |
| U. Jeremy Roenick | *U* | JR |
| V. Brad McCrimmon | *L* | Moose |
| W. Bill Flett | | Cookie |
| X. Simon Gagne | *N* | The Count |
| Y. Dominic Roussel | *V* | The Beast |
| Z. Kjell Samuelsson | *M* | Big Bird |

114

# 5 PLAYOFF GAMES THAT
# I WILL NEVER FORGET

*While there are many memorable Flyers' games that could have appeared on this list, the following five contests epitomize Philadelphia hockey. Though some of the outcomes were heart-wrenching, that's simply the life of a Flyers' fan.*

***5. May 28, 1987…Game 6 of the 1987 Stanley Cup Finals versus the Edmonton Oilers***

Though I can't tell you first-hand, the Spectrum was loud that fateful 1987 night. I was indeed in the heart of South Philadelphia's sports complex that evening; however, instead of cheering on the Flyers at the Spectrum, I was enjoying the Genesis concert across the street at Veterans Stadium.

The decision between the game and concert was a difficult one, but it ultimately came down to a simple fact: I couldn't stomach watching Wayne Gretzky and Mark Messier carry Lord Stanley's silver chalice on Spectrum ice. They didn't. All while the musicians preformed, Brian Propp and JJ Daigneault were energizing the crowd of 17,222 with their tying and game-winning goals - just 1:24 apart.

# FLYER'D UP!

Trivia, Facts, and Anecdotes for Fans of the Orange and Black.

The Flyers won the game 3-2, which forced Game 7 in Edmonton. They ultimately lost there, but I still regret my decision to attend the concert. I remember the show mostly for my feelings during all of the great songs and drum solos. My heart was across the street at those times; instead of enjoying the music, I was wondering how my team was faring. When Phil Collins announced that the Flyers had gone ahead in the third period, I missed the game even more. Each of the 28 times I watched the tape that night, I wished harder that I had chosen hockey.

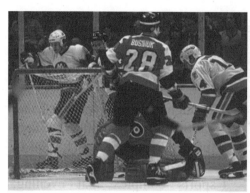

### 4. May 24, 1980...Game 6 of the 1980 Stanley Cup Finals versus the New York Islanders

The "Leon Stickle" game (as it is known to many Flyers' fans) hurt. Though I was only nine years old in 1980, I had already developed as a Flyers fan.

I enjoyed the 1979-1980 season. I relished in the 35 game unbeaten streak and the playoff victories over the Edmonton Oilers, New York Rangers, and Minnesota North Stars. I believed, like many Flyer faithful, that Philadelphia would be home to the Stanley Cup at the conclusion of the playoffs. Only the New York Islanders stood in the way of Philadelphia's collective hope. Though the Flyers trailed the series three games to two, I thought that they would be strong enough to come away with a win in Uniondale, New York.

The stage was set at Nassau County Veterans Memorial Coliseum for Game

*Did you know that the Flyers have an all-time winning record against every franchise in the NHL except for the Montreal Canadiens and Boston Bruins? (They do have losing records versus the Colorado Avalanche, New Jersey Devils and Dallas Stars, but hold the cumulative all –time winning advantage when factoring in wins versus Quebec (Colorado), Kansas City and Colorado (New Jersey) and Minnesota (Dallas)*

# FLYER'D UP!

Trivia, Facts, and Anecdotes for Fans of the Orange and Black.

6 on that May afternoon. All of Philadelphia was prepared for a victory, and it came awfully close to being right. As the drama unfolded, the Flyers fought back from a 4-2 deficit in the third period, getting goals from Bob Dailey and John Paddock to force overtime. Seven minutes into the first extra period, the Islanders' Bob Nystrom had beat Flyers' goaltender Pete Peeters for the game-winning goal - and the Stanley Cup. There was one problem with the victory: Nystrom had been offside. Linesman Leon Stickle had neglected to make the call. I, like many Flyer fans, were left both outraged and heartbroken.

A few years ago while attending a game in New York, I ran into Clarke Gillies, Nystrom's teammate on the Islanders for many years. Over a few beers, we discussed hockey. Not surprisingly, the game - and the call - came up in our conversation. While he admitted that Nystrom was offside, he good-naturedly told me to move on. I did, temporarily - or at least until the booze wore off.

### 3. May 4 2000…. Game 4 of the 2000 Eastern Conference Finals versus the Pittsburgh Penguins.

As far as epic sports battles go, this was one for the record books. As one of the longest games in NHL history, Game 4 of the 2000 Eastern Conference Finals is remembered by not only Flyer and Penguin fans, but also by those who love sports. That evening, the Flyers trailed the series two games to one and

# FLYER'D UP!

Trivia, Facts, and Anecdotes for Fans of the Orange and Black.

were in Pittsburgh to even the score.

I listened to the first two periods on a radio in a softball dugout and then decided to join my team at a local bar to watch the third period. The softball team and I were lucky enough to see John LeClair tie the game with a power play goal; however, after the first overtime, we went our separate ways.

I arrived home in the middle of the second overtime and then, for the next two and a half hours, sat on the end of my coffee table, biting my nails. That night, the battle between the Flyers and Penguins became an instant classic. It finally finished at 12:01 of the fifth overtime when Keith Primeau ripped a wrist shot over the glove of Penguins goaltender ~~Ken Wregget~~. The goal ended the third longest game in NHL history and kept the Flyers' playoff hopes alive for another day. *RON TUGNUTT*

While the game ended at 2:35 AM on the east coast, Flyers fans were awake and overjoyed. The enthusiasm was not in vain: for once, there was a happy ending for Philadelphia. The Flyers used the momentum from the grueling match to eventually win the series in six games.

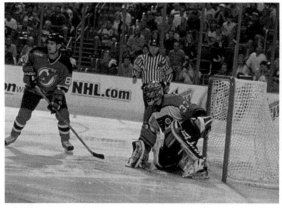

## 2. May 26, 2000...Game 7 of the 2000 Eastern Conference Finals versus the New Jersey Devils.

This 2000 playoff loss against the New Jersey Devils was, perhaps the most devastating I had ever encountered as a Flyers fan. When I was in East Rutherford following

# FLYER'D UP!

Trivia, Facts, and Anecdotes for Fans of the Orange and Black.

Game 4 at the Continental Arena, I celebrated. That day, I felt good about the Flyers' chances - I thought they could bring home a Stanley Cup. They had just dominated the Devils in a 3-1 victory to take a commanding three games to one series advantage. They were one win away from another shot at the Cup. After celebrating, however, I made my way home that evening. By the time I had arrived in South Jersey, I knew that the Devils were going to fight back. Sure enough, I had been right.

The Devils won the next two games. They even beat the Flyers in Game 6, when Eric Lindros returned to the ice after an extended absence following a series of concussions. While Lindros, scoring the only Flyers' goal, outshone his teammates, many fans worried that his return would disrupt the team's flawless chemistry. The Devils won the game 2-1 and the two teams returned to Philadelphia for Game 7.

Though Game 7 was close (tied at one goal apiece as the clock ticked down in the third period), the building was distracted. Just 7:50 into the game, the Devils' Scott Stevens checked Lindros at the Devils' blue line. At the time of the check, Lindros had his head down - he never saw Stevens coming. He remained unconscious for several minutes, during which time fans held their breath. Lindros eventually recovered, but he never played another minute in a Flyers uniform.

Patrick Elias scored the game-winner with 2:32 remaining in the game. The Devils had erased the series deficit. It would be the New Jersey team, not the Flyers, who would take on the Dallas Stars for the Stanley Cup.

I left the Wachovia Center crushed. The game not only ended a season, but also an era.

# FLYER'D UP!

Trivia, Facts, and Anecdotes for Fans of the Orange and Black.

### *1. May 4, 2004…Game 6 of the Eastern Conference Semi Finals versus the Toronto Maple Leafs*

On this early May evening in 2004, I was in New York City on business. The best nights of my stay at the Fitzpatrick Hotel were those that included Flyers playoff hockey. I may have been in Ranger territory, but it didn't stop me from enjoying the action on a company dime.

I set up for a special night in my hotel room. I didn't have plans to go to a New York bar because, after all, I was a Flyers fan. Around 5 PM, I purchased a 12-pack of Heineken, 12 hot wings, and a bacon cheeseburger.

**5 Playoff Games that I will Never Forget**

# FLYER'D UP!

Trivia, Facts, and Anecdotes for Fans of the Orange and Black.

Tonight, I just knew that I would be celebrating.

The game didn't disappoint. The Flyers led 2-0 in the first period, due to goals by Radovan Somik and Jeremy Roenick. The score remained that way until halfway through the third period, when the Leafs scored two goals in just over six minutes. The game was headed into overtime.

The Flyers controlled early overtime play. Flyers goaltender Robert Esche kept the Leafs out of the game with amazing saves; however, I haven't yet forgotten the playoff action that followed. In the first overtime, Flyers forward Sammi Kapanen was leveled by Darcy Tucker. The hit was devastating; it knocked Kapanen clear into the next round, exactly where the Flyers were headed. Following Tucker's blow, Kapanen stumbled on his skates to the bench.

Moments later, Roenick flew down the right wing into the Leafs zone on a two-on-one with Tony Amonte, but everyone watching knew Roenick had shooting on his mind. He unleashed a wicked wrist shot that beat Ed Belfour and officially sent the Flyers to another Eastern Conference Final.

Following the exciting victory, I donned my Flyers jersey and began to smoke a victory cigar. As I confidently walked into the hotel bar, I smiled. While Ranger fans were bitter, I was overwhelmed with happiness. I loved the moment.

# FLYER'D UP!

## THE NUMBERS GAME

1. Which of the following Flyers did NOT wear number 3?
A. Garry Galley     B. Doug Crossman     C. Behn Wilson     D. Frank Bathe

2. Which of the following Flyers did NOT wear number 5?
A. Rob Ramage     B. Kevin Haller     C. Nolan Baumgartner     D. Mattias Timander

3. Daryl Stanley wore all of the following numbers as a Flyer except:
A. 28           B. 8           C. 29           D. 34

4. Dennis Ververgaert wore all of the following numbers as a Flyer except:
A. 11           B. 27           C. 28           D. 43

5. All of the Flyers wore the # 8 except:
A. Brad Marsh     B. Dave Hoyda     C. Geoff Sanderson     D. Mike Peluso

6. Rick MacLeish wore # 19 as a member of the 1974 Stanley Cup Champion Flyers, what number did he wear when he returned in 1983?
A. 20           B. 21           C. 22           D. 29

7. Petr Svoboda wore two numbers for Flyers during his career, which were they?
A. 3 & 23       B. 3 &33       C. 13 & 23       D. 3 &13

8. Which number did Brad McCrimmon wear while a member of the Flyers?
A. 12           B. 8           C. 10           D. 2

9. Which two of the following players wore #13 for the Flyers
A. Ken Linesman     B. Dave Michayluk     C. Claude Lapointe     D. Magnus Roupe

10. All of the following Flyers wore number 7 after Bill Barber retired in 1985 except:
A. Craig Fisher     B. Brian Dobbin     C. Glen Seabrooke     D. Jay Wells

11. Defenseman Reid Bailey played for the Flyers from 1980-82. How many different numbers did he wear for the orange and black?
A. 1           B. 2           C) 3           D) 4

122

answers on page 180

# FLYER'D UP!

Trivia, Facts, and Anecdotes for Fans of the Orange and Black.

# THE NUMBERS GAME

12. Which of these Flyers did not wear number 12?
A. Tim Kerr     B. Jiri Latal     C. Gary Dornhoefer     D. Patrik Juhlin

13. Chris Therien wore the number 6 jersey for the Flyers for his entire Flyers' career. Which jersey number did he wear first in pre-season before being permanently assigned number 6?
A. 41          B. 56          C. 40          D. 58

14. Bernie Parent's #1 hangs from the rafters of the Wachovia Center and is retired by the Flyers. Which number did Parent first wear for the Flyers?
A. 33          B. 35          C. 30          D. 27

15. Defenseman Jason Bowen was assigned four numbers during his 1992-97 Flyers' career. Which of the following numbers did he NOT wear?
A. 28          B. 53          C. 19          D. 8

16. Craig Berube wore four different numbers for the Flyers during two different stints with the team. Which of the following did he NOT wear?
A. 17          B. 12          C. 32          D. 8

17. Who was the first-ever Flyer to wear number 24?
A. Terry Ball     B. Lou Angotti     C. John Hanna     D. Pat Hannigan

18. All of the following players have worn number 18 for the Flyers EXCEPT:
A. Ross Lonsberry     B. Paul Lawless     C. Lindsay Carson     D. Nick Fotiu

19. All of the following Flyers have worn number 55 EXCEPT:
A. Chris Gratton     B. Paul Coffey     C. Ben Eager     D. Ulf Samuelsson

20. Which of the following Flyers NEVER wore number 2 for the orange and black?
A. Adam Burt     B. Mark Howe     C. Dmitri Tertyshny     D. Ed Van Impe

123

**answers on page 180**

# FLYER'D UP!

Trivia, Facts, and Anecdotes for Fans of the Orange and Black.

# MOST UNDERRATED FLYERS
### By Al Morganti

*Al Morganti is a hockey analyst who has covered the NHL as well as international competitions. Currently, he covers the Flyers for Comcast Sportsnet and is a colleague of mine at Sportsradio610 WIP where he co-hosts The Morning Show with Angelo Cataldi.*

*1) Eric Desjardins* - As one of the toughest guys to play for the team, Desjardins played hurt without issue. The team relied on him, regardless of the situation. No matter how much the Flyers tried to limit his ice time, he was used a workhorse from October through the end of the season.

*2) Mark Howe* - Though he was not necessarily underrated as a Flyer, he definitely did not receive his due credit from the National Hockey League. Mark Howe deserved a better spot in League history.

*3) Eric Lindros* - The off ice issues -- and there were many -- cloud the fact that Lindros was the real deal. He was tough and talented and a very underrated passer. Unfortunately, he never reaped the benefits of his talent in Philadelphia.

*4) Dave Brown -* Yes, Brownie could throw hands. More importantly, however, he was the ultimate team guy. The Flyers could count on Brown to unselfishly succeed in his role on the ice, which, oftentimes, was the most difficult task.

5) (tie) *Chris Therien and Craig Berube* - Therien played many years in many games in an organization that is so demanding -- and they brought him back. As for Berube, every team that had him on their roster wanted to keep him there.

# FLYER'D UP!

## THE STREAK

1. Who was the only team in the NHL in 1979-80 whom the Flyers didn't face during their 35 game unbeaten streak?
A. Washington Capitals    B. Montreal Canadiens
C. Chicago Blackhawks    D. Atlanta Flames

2. Before the Flyers set the mark for the longest unbeaten streak in North American sports' history, who held the record?
A. Los Angeles Lakers    B. Boston Celtics
C. Dallas Cowboys    D. Montreal Canadiens

3. Which NHL team held the previous record for most games without a loss prior to the Flyers 1979-80 season?
A. Boston Bruins    B. Detroit Red Wings
C. Montreal Canadiens    D. Toronto Maple Leafs

4. Which team defeated the Flyers to end the unbeaten streak at 35?
A. Chicago Blackhawks    B. Minnesota North Stars
C. Atlanta Flames    D. Pittsburgh Penguins

5. Who was the last team to beat the Flyers before they went 35 straight without a loss?
A. New York Islanders    B. New York Rangers
C. Boston Bruins    D. Atlanta Flames

6. In game #29 of the streak, the Flyers broke the previous NHL record for consecutive games without a loss. Who was the Flyers opponent?
A. Buffalo Sabres    B. Vancouver Canucks
C. Boston Bruins    D. Atlanta Flames

 **Most Underrated Flyers**

answers on page 180

# FLYER'D UP!

Trivia, Facts, and Anecdotes for Fans of the Orange and Black.

# THE STREAK

7. Whom did the Flyers defeat in game #35 of the streak?
A. Buffalo Sabres        B. Hartford Whalers
C. Quebec Nordiques      D. Montreal Canadiens

8. How many victories did the Flyers earn during the 35 game unbeaten streak?
A. 24                    B. 26
C. 29                    D. 25

9. How many games had the Flyers played prior to the start of the streak?
A. 2                     B. 6
C. 3                     D. 4

10. Which two goaltenders recorded victories for the team during the streak?
A. Phil Myre             B. Robbie Moore
C. Pete Peeters          D. Rick St. Croix

11. Who was the first Flyers' defenseman to record a game-winning goal during the streak?
A. Behn Wilson           B. Norm Barnes
C. Frank Bathe           D. Bob Dailey

12. What was the Flyers' longest previous unbeaten streak before 1979-80?
A. 22                    B. 19
C. 17                    D. 23

13. How many times were the Flyers out-shot during the streak?
A. 1                     B. 2
C. 8                     D. 12

127

**answers on page 180**

# FLYER'D UP!

Trivia, Facts, and Anecdotes for Fans of the Orange and Black.

14. Who was the Flyers' head coach at the time of the 35-game unbeaten streak?
A. Bob McCammon          B. Fred Shero
C. Pat Quinn             D. Mike Keenan

15. During game #28, the Flyers trailed the Pittsburgh Penguins 1-0 late in the third period. Who scored the game-tying goal to extend the streak?
A. Ken Linesman          B. Reggie Leach
C. Brian Propp           D. Behn Wilson

16. During game #23 of the streak, which player's 2 second period goals in 20 seconds kicked of a string of 9 consecutive goals against the Los Angeles Kings?
A) Bobby Clarke          B) Bill Barber
C) Brian Propp           D) Reggie Leach

*The Flyers celebrate their record setting 29th consecutive game unbeaten at Boston Garden December 22, 1979. The streak would continue on to a still standing record of 35 games.*

# FLYER'D UP!

Trivia, Facts, and Anecdotes for Fans of the Orange and Black.

# THE PLAYER'S MOST UNDERRATED LIST

*Throughout interviews I've seen and conducted with Flyers players from 1967 until today, I discovered that most of those who wore the orange and black didn't buy into the individual labels of overrated or underrated. It was the success of the team as a whole that mattered most. Below is a compilation of quotes and opinions from recent player interviews that were conducted on the topic of the most underrated players to ever wear the Flyers uniform as seen through their eyes.*

### Brad Marsh
"For me it had to be the fighters and the heavyweights. For instance, Glen Cochrane was a good defenseman and was tough as nails. He didn't fight just to fight, he fought for his teammates, and brought a lot to the team.

"On the offensive side, Dave Pouilin was a tremendous captain, but what people didn't realize was how gifted he was on both ends of the ice. He came from out of nowhere to be a pretty darn good forward and was flat out incredible when it came to defensive play."

### Ron Sutter
"It's all about the unsung heroes, the guys on the third and fourth lines that bought into the system; and I know for a fact that the top-end guys always showed appreciation for the lower-end guys because they knew all along it was those guys that put them into a position to score and win."

*Did you know that Dave Shultz was whistled for an NHL record 472 penalty minutes during the 1974-75 season?*

# FLYER'D UP!

Trivia, Facts, and Anecdotes for Fans of the Orange and Black.

### Brad "The Beast" McCrimmon

"Well, we focused on the team so a lot flew under the radar. Mark Howe should have won several Norris Trophies and never did. Brian Propp was a great two-way player who did everything but never got his due. Ron Sutter should have won a Selke Trophy, but the focus was our team and that's why it was so special. And another thing, if Dave Poulin was on the ice, his opponents were a minus three -- I guarantee it. "

### Bobby "Chief" Taylor

"[The most underrated] had to be Ross Lonsberry. He scored 30 plus every year; he did all the checking for MacLeish and Dornhoefer; [he] was responsible defensively and he knew how to score. He'd be making 9 million per year now.

"Also, when it comes to offensively gifted guys, look no further than the big-game mentality that Rick MacLeish had. Game 7 in 1975, he scored a hat trick versus the Islanders that won us the series."

### Lou Angotti, Flyers First Captain

"Ed Van Impe [is the most underrated player] by far; it's not even close. A lot of people don't know that he finished second behind Bobby Orr for the Calder Trophy. When the Flyers traded him to Pittsburgh, his presence was missed -- I guarantee that. He came to work every day and was as tough as nails."

### Bill Clement

"I think Orest Kindrachuk fits the bill. He went into the corners; he was durable, a hard worker. And I remember in '75 in the Finals against the Sabres, he took both Jerry Korab and Lee Fogolin's hits and passed me the puck when I scored our second goal that game. He wasn't the prettiest skater, and he doesn't get many points for style, but he was a contributor."

## FLYER'D UP!

Trivia, Facts, and Anecdotes for Fans of the Orange and Black.

### Keith Jones

"Eric Desjardins. He was good enough to win the Norris, and it's no coincidence the Flyers had their worst year in 2006 when he retired. He was that important."

### Craig Berube

"Dave Poulin would be my choice. ]He was a] great captain, teammate, friend, player [and] leader. He was a way better player than people gave him credit for."

### Ron Hextall

"Eric Desjardins was unbelievable - so much better than everybody thought. [He] should have won a Norris along with Mark Howe -- two guys that played within their team limits and were never rewarded with personal trophies."

### Orest Kindrachuck

"Ross Lonsberry was so important to our success as a team. What a great work ethic, great attitude and no excuses. He played the game harder than anybody, and he knew how to do it."

### Dave Brown

"That's simple: Mark Howe. He should be in the NHL Hall of Fame."

### Mark Howe

"Of the players I played with, it was Brian Propp and Brad McCrimmon. I know how good Propp was because I had the great opportunity to play with him for many years. He was irreplaceable to the team. And Brad was never given the credit he deserved when he and I were partners on defense. We were a plus 190 in three years together as defensive partners for the Flyers.

# FLYER'D UP!

Trivia, Facts, and Anecdotes for Fans of the Orange and Black.

That can't be accomplished without two players playing as one. We were a great pair but unfortunately in the media, I received mostly all of the credit - but I knew differently."

### Bob "Hound" Kelly

"The guys on the blue line during our 35 game unbeaten streak: Frank Bathe, Mike Busniuk [and] Norm Barnes. That defense was great. No one knew who the "three B's" were, but [the team] sure did."

### Gary Dornhoefer

"It was Orest Kindrachuk. When you watched him play, he was the best hanging on to the puck and not giving it away when the heat was on. I had a lot of respect for the way in which he played the game."

### Brian Propp

"Mark Howe was the most underrated Flyer of all time. He should have won the Norris Trophy at least three times."

### Peter Zezel

"Mark Howe. He should have won many awards."

### Consensus:

Defensemen Eric Desjardins and Mark Howe were the most underrated Flyers in the organization's history. With all due respect to Rico, this analyst's choice is Mark Howe.

*Two great defensemen, Eric Desjardins and Mark Howe*

# FLYER'D UP!

Trivia, Facts, and Anecdotes for Fans of the Orange and Black.

Perhaps being the son of one of the greatest players to wear an NHL uniform in Gordie Howe clouded memories for some, but for former Flyers teammates, fans, writers and broadcasters alike, Howe is the clear choice. He was indeed one of a kind.

Howe was acquired by the Flyers in a blockbuster deal with the Hartford Whalers in the summer of 1982. The Flyers gave up Greg Adams, Ken Linesman and their first- and third-round draft picks in 1983. They could've thrown in three more first-rounders and the Whalers still would have been fleeced. Howe's incredible mix of offensive flair, combined with his smooth skating and defensive shut-down capabilities were the backbone of the Flyers success. He was simply amazing and a class act to boot, always giving the credit to his teammates. As many have stated, Howe should have skated away with several Norris Trophies, but in the end was only a finalist three times. Though the lack of accolades was a travesty to most who know the game of hockey, to Howe, it was clearly not important.

"Mark never cared about trying to compete for the most points by a defenseman. He didn't care if he ever won the Norris Trophy. He just cared about the Flyers winning games," said former teammate Dave Poulin. "If you look at our teams in the 1980s, we had a lot of good players, but Mark Howe is the only one who probably belongs in the Hall of Fame."

In 594 games in the orange and black, Howe recorded 138 goals and 342 assists for 480 points. These totals were good enough to place him as the Flyers all-time leading scorer amongst defenseman and thirteenth overall on the franchise's all-time list. He may have never won a major award or the Stanley Cup, but will forever be remembered as one of the greatest Flyers of all time. He was that good.

**The Player's Most Underrated List**  133

*Did you know that during the Flyers 35 game unbeaten streak in the 1979-80 season, the Washington Capitals were the only team the Flyers did not face?*

# FLYER'D UP!

## TRADES TRIVIA

1. Who was the first Flyer ever traded?
A. Rick MacLeish          B. Lew Morrison
C. Wayne Hicks            D. Art Stratton

2. In March of 1976, the Flyers traded Bobby Taylor and Ed Van Impe to the Pittsburgh Penguins in exchange for whom?
A. Gary Inness            B. Wayne Stephenson
C. Denis Heron            D. Larry Goodenough

3. Who was the first player the Flyers ever obtained through a trade?
A. Rosarie Paiment        B. Reggie Fleming
C. Rick MacLeish          D. Ed Van Impe

4. When the Flyers traded Mel Bridgman to the Calgary Flames in 1981, which defenseman did they acquire?
A. Miro Dvorak            B. Behn Wilson
C. Brad Marsh             D. Mark Howe

5. Which two players were traded to the Winnipeg Jets in 1989 only to be returned to the Flyers five days later?
A. Pete Peeters and Andrei Lomakin    B. Bill Root and Greg Smyth
C. Pete Peeters and Keith Acton       D. Keith Acton and Dave Brown

6. Who did the Flyers receive from the Boston Bruins in the 1990 trade of Dave Poulin?
A. Bill Root              B. Jay Wells
C. Kevin Maguire          D. Ken Linesman

7. Which of the following players was NOT involved in the Flyers' trade for the rights to Eric Lindros?
A. Kerry Huffman          B. Steve Duchesne
C. Chris Simon            D. Brent Fedyk

8. The Flyers traded Pelle Eklund to which team?
A. Edmonton Oilers        B. St. Louis Blues
C. Dallas Stars           D. Hartford Whalers

9. When the Flyers acquired Dale Hawerchuk from the St. Louis Blues in 1996, whom did they trade?
A. Peter Zezel            B. Craig MacTavish
C. Murray Baron           D. Mike Bullard

134

**answers on page 180**

# FLYER'D UP!

Trivia, Facts, and Anecdotes for Fans of the Orange and Black.

## TRADES TRIVIA

10. From which team did the Flyers acquire Terry Murray in 1977?
A. Detroit Red Wings          B. Montreal Canadiens
C. Washington Capitals        D. Buffalo Sabres

11. The Flyers traded Mark Recchi to the Montreal Canadiens for all of these players EXCEPT:
A. John Leclair               B. Kevin Haller
C. Gilbert Dionne             D. Eric Desjardins

12. Whom did the Flyers trade to Colorado for the rights to Keith Jones?
A. Shjon Podein               B. Joel Otto
C. Daniel Lacroix             D. Mike Maneluk

13. To which team did the Flyers trade Michal Handzus?
A. Chicago Blackhawks         B. St. Louis Blues
C. New York Rangers           D. Los Angeles Kings

14. To which team did the Flyers trade Joe Watson in 1978?
A. Pittsburgh Penguins        B. Colorado Rockies
C. Cleveland Barons           D. Washington Capitals

15. Who did the Flyers receive as part of the trade that sent Bernie Parent to the Boston Bruins in 1971?
A. Bruce Gamble               B. Rick MacLeish
C. Larry Hillman              D. Larry Mickey

16. Who was the first player the Flyers received from the Pittsburgh Penguins in a trade?
A. Wayne Hicks                B. Dave Schultz
C. Bob Kelly                  D. Art Stratton

17. Which other Flyer accompanied Bruno St. Jaques in a 2003 trade to the Carolina Hurricanes that brought Sami Kapanen and Ryan Bast to the Flyers?
A. Justin Williams            B. Danny Markov
C. Pavel Brendl               D. Paul Ranheim

18. The Flyers traded Chris Gratton and Mike Sillinger to the Tampa Bay Lightning for Mikael Renberg and whom in 1998?
A. Peter Svoboda              B. Karl Dykhuis
C. Daymond Langkow            D. Alexandre Daigle

135

**answers on page 180**

# FLYER'D UP!

Trivia, Facts, and Anecdotes for Fans of the Orange and Black.

## TRADES TRIVIA

19. Rick Tocchet was traded to the Pittsburgh Penguins in 1992 and re-acquired in 2000 from which organization?
A. Washington Capitals
B. Phoenix Coyotes
C. Pittsburgh Penguins
D. Boston Bruins

20. When the Flyers traded Coach Fred Shero in 1978 to the New York Rangers, they received a first-round pick that turned out to be whom?
A. Blake Dunlop
B. Glen Wesley
C. Drew Callander
D. Ken Linesman

21. The Flyers traded Behn Wilson to the Chicago Blackhawks for a first-round pick and which player?
A. Doug Crossman
B. Doug Wilson
C. Gordie Roberts
D. Ed Hospodar

22. The Flyers received Joe Patterson and Murray Craven from the Detroit Red Wings in a 1984 trade. Who did they trade?
A. Darryl Sittler
B. Glen Cochrane
C. Len Hachborn
D. Mark Laforest

23. Peter Zezel was traded to the St. Louis Blues in 1988 for Mike Bullard. To which team did the Flyers trade Mike Bullard in 1991?
A. Buffalo Sabres
B. Detroit Red Wings
C. Toronto Maple Leafs
D. New York Rangers

24. Whom did the Flyers receive for trading the rights to Lindsay Carson in 1988?
A. Paul Guay
B. Paul Lawless
C. Gordie Roberts
D. Mike Stothers

25. Which of the following players was not included in the return from the New York Rangers for the rights to Eric Lindros?
A. Jan Hlavac
B. Kim Johnsson
C. Pavel Brendl
D. Peter Hubacek

**answers on page 180**

# FLYER'D UP!

Trivia, Facts, and Anecdotes for Fans of the Orange and Black.

# BEST COACHES IN FLYERS HISTORY
## By Glen Macnow

*Glen Macnow has been a host on Sportsradio 610WIP for 15 years. Before he was a broadcaster, Macnow was a sportswriter for the Philadelphia Inquirer. He has written more than 15 books, including three extremely popular titles: The Great Philadelphia Fan Book, The Great Philadelphia Sports Debate and, most recently, The Great Book of Philadelphia Sports Lists. Macnow has also shared in hosting the pre- and post-game shows of Philadelphia Flyers hockey. He is a huge fan of the game.*

*Flyers head coach Fred Shero behind the bench*

***1. Fred Shero, 1971-78.*** How can there be an argument against Shero? He holds the franchise records for most regular-season wins (308), playoff wins (42) and career winning percentage (.642). He also coached the Broad

# FLYER'D UP!

Trivia, Facts, and Anecdotes for Fans of the Orange and Black.

Street Bullies to the only two Stanley Cups in the town's history, in 1974 and 1975.

His players called him "The Fog," a title that was not meant to disparage but to recognize that his mind was often elsewhere. The coach was constantly trying to concoct new ways to win. During a game in his first season, Shero disappeared during an intermission and was not on the bench when play resumed. Turned out that Shero, lost in thought, started wandering during the break and locked himself out of the arena.

Shero was known for his brilliant aphorisms ("Be like a duck," he once wrote on the locker room chalkboard. "Keep calm and unruffled on the surface, but paddle like hell underneath."). Sometimes his players understood his writings; sometimes they just scratched their heads.
On May 19, 1974, he wrote his most famous saying: "Win today and we walk together forever." They did.

***2. Mike Keenan, 1984-88***. Keenan made two appearances in the Stanley Cup Finals in 1985 and 1987. Though he ultimately lost both times, it was forgivable: the victor was an Edmonton Oilers franchise that may be the most complete team in league history. Keenan was a devotee of the great Scotty Bowman, and coached like his hero – right down to the scowl he carried on the bench.

"Iron Mike" coached in a way that sometimes confused both fans and players. Example: During a first-round game in the 1987 playoffs, he switched goalies – from Ron Hextall to Chico Resch – five times. Neither had played poorly, Keenan just wanted to keep everyone on their toes.

 **Best Coaches in Flyers History**

*Did you know that the Flyers have had 4 different players with the surname Murray play for them? The most of any last name. (Marty, Mike, Pat and Terry)*

# FLYER'D UP!

Trivia, Facts, and Anecdotes for Fans of the Orange and Black.

Keenan's success came from his organization, motivation and intimidation. Ultimately, his bullying tactics turned off his players. Truth be told, most of the team despised him. After losing in the first round of the 1988 playoffs, he was fired. As they watched in disbelief, Flyer fans were obviously unhappy when Keenan coached the New York Rangers to a Cup in 1994.

*3. Ken Hitchcock, 2002-06.* A thinking man's coach and a favorite of Flyers fans, "Hitch" guided the Flyers to the Eastern Conference Finals in 2004. If the team hadn't lost three regular defensemen to injury, it had a real chance to get to the Stanley Cup Finals.

Hitchcock demanded much from his players, both in practices and in games. He would fume at anyone who refused to skate back on defense and stare down a skater who carelessly gave away a puck. But his demand for excellence usually paid off.

Beyond that, Hitch knew how to talk to fans. He gave enlightened news conferences and didn't mind giving erudite answers, even to dumb questions. Man, we could use a few more coaches like that in this town.

*4. Pat Quinn, 1978-82.* Quinn was at the helm in 1979-80 when the Flyers went 35 straight games without a loss -- a league record. The team finished first that season before losing to the New York Islander dynasty in the 1980 Finals. If not for linesman Leon Stickle, Quinn and the Flyer team would have sipped champagne from the big trophy that year.

# FLYER'D UP!

Trivia, Facts, and Anecdotes for Fans of the Orange and Black.

Quinn was big and tough as a player, and carried that demeanor to the bench. He also believed in team camaraderie, sometimes walking his team from the Spectrum to nearby Roosevelt Park after practice for a game of soccer.

**5. John Stevens, 2006- .** You were expecting Terry Simpson, maybe? This may be an optimistic pick, but after suffering through a terrible first season in 2006-07 (which wasn't Stevens' fault – injuries, combined with a pathetic roster, pushed the Flyers to the bottom of the standings), Stevens showed an ability to learn on the fly in 2007-08. He shifted lines, instructed young defenseman and inspired goalie Martin Biron to play the best hockey of his career. And the Flyers – shock of shocks – reached the Eastern Conference Finals.

Here's to hoping that Stevens can continue his success with the team and perhaps push his name further up the list of great Flyers' coaches in the coming years.

### FLYERS COACHING RECORDS 1967-2008

| | COACH | FIRST SEASON | NO. OF SEASONS | | RECORD | | PCT. | PLAYOFF RECORD | | PLAYOFF PCT. |
|---|---|---|---|---|---|---|---|---|---|---|
| | Keith Allen | 1967-68 | 2 | 51 | • 67 • | 32 | .447 | 3 • | 8 | .273 |
| | Vic Stasiuk | 1969-70 | 2 | 45 | • 68 • | 41 | .425 | 0 • | 4 | .000 |
| | Fred Shero | 1971-72 | 7 | 308 | • 151 • | 95 | .642 | 48 • | 35 | .578 |
| # | Bob McCammon | 1978-79 | 4 | 119 | • 68 • | 31 | .617 | 1 • | 9 | .100 |
| * | Pat Quinn | 1978-79 | 4 | 141 | • 73 • | 48 | .630 | 22 • | 17 | .564 |
| | Mike Keenan | 1984-85 | 4 | 190 | • 102 • | 28 | .638 | 32 • | 25 | .561 |
| | Paul Holmgren | 1988-89 | 4 | 107 | • 126 • | 31 | .464 | 10 • | 9 | .526 |
| @ | Bill Dineen | 1991-92 | 2 | 60 | • 60 • | 20 | .500 | — | | — |
| | Terry Simpson | 1993-94 | 1 | 35 | • 39 • | 10 | .476 | — | | — |
| | Terry Murray | 1994-95 | 3 | 118 | • 64 • | 30 | .627 | 28 • | 18 | .609 |
| | Wayne Cashman | 1997-98 | 1 | 32 | • 20 • | 9 | .598 | — | | — |
| + | Roger Neilson | 1997-98 | 3 | 76 | • 52 • | 32 | .578 | 3 • | 8 | .273 |
| % | Craig Ramsay | 1999-2000 | 2 | 28 | • 20 • | 5 | .594 | 11 • | 7 | .611 |
| ^ | Bill Barber | 2000-01 | 2 | 73 | • 46 • | 17 | .599 | 3 • | 8 | .273 |
| | Ken Hitchcock | 2002-03 | 3 | 130 | • 77 • | 39 | .608 | 19 • | 18 | .514 |
| > | John Stevens | 2006-07 | 2 | 63 | • 71 • | 22 | .474 | 9 • | 8 | .529 |

**Best Coaches in Flyers History**

```
*   Replaced Bob McCammon 50 games into the 1978-79 season, compiling an 18-8-4 mark.
#   Replaced Pat Quinn 72 games into the 1981-82 season, compiling a 4-2-2 mark.
@   Replaced Paul Holmgren 24 games into the 1991-92 season, compiling a 24-23-9 mark.
+   Replaced Wayne Cashman 61 games into the 1997-98 season, compiling a 10-9-2 mark.
%   Replaced Roger Neilson 57 games into the 1999-2000 season, compiling a 16-8-1 mark.
^   Replaced Craig Ramsay 28 games into the 2000-01 season, compiling a 31-16-7 mark.
>   Replaced Ken Hitchcock 8 games into the 2006-07 season, compiling a 21-42-11 mark.
```

# FLYER'D UP!

Trivia, Facts, and Anecdotes for Fans of the Orange and Black.

## FLYERS HEAD COACHES WORD SEARCH

```
Q O B N I O L O N N N
U N A B S N E V E T S
I I R S A O O R L I H
N N B N I M G S L O E
N E E A O M T Q A C R
O E R E L A P N A S O
K N S O S C U S S A A
T I H I T C H C O C K
S D U R A M S E Y N I
E K H Y A R R U M S B
N R M N E I L S O N S
```

| | | |
|---|---|---|
| ALLEN | STASIUK | SHERO |
| MCCAMMON | QUINN | KEENAN |
| HOLMGREN | DINEEN | SIMPSON |
| MURRAY | CASHMAN | NEILSON |
| RAMSEY | BARBER | HITCHCOCK |
| STEVENS | | |

answers on page 182

# FLYER'D UP!

Trivia, Facts, and Anecdotes for Fans of the Orange and Black.

## BOBBY CLARKE TRIVIA

1. How many career hat tricks did Bobby Clarke score with the Flyers?
A. 5          B. 9          C. 12.          D. 17

2. Who were Bobby Clarke's linemates during his first season playing for the Flyers?
A. Lew Morrison/Reggie Fleming          B. Bill Barber/Reggie Leach
C. Gary Dornhoefer/Bill Barber          D. Bill Flett/Simon Nolet

3. The Flyers have retired number 16 in honor of Bobby Clarke. Which of the following players also wore number 16?
A. Pat Hannigan          B. Claude LaForge
C. Don Blackburn          D. John Miszuk

4. When he became General Manager of the Flyers, whom did Bob Clarke hire as his first head coach?
A. Paul Holmgren          B. Terry Murray
C. Pat Quinn          D. Mike Keenan

5. Against which team did Bobby Clarke play his last NHL game as a Flyer?
A. Pittsburgh Penguins          B. Calgary Flames
C. Vancouver Canucks          D. Washington Capitals

6. How many games did Bobby Clarke play for the Philadelphia Flyers?
A. 978          B. 1144          C. 1273          D. 1472

7. Who was the first Flyers' player traded by GM Bobby Clarke?
A. Darryl Sittler          B. Sam St. Laurent
C. Murray Caven          D. Scott Mellanby

8. Bobby Clarke led the 1975-76 Flyers in points. How many did he have?
A. 120          B. 119          C. 118          D. 124

142

answers on page 180

# FLYER'D UP!

Trivia, Facts, and Anecdotes for Fans of the Orange and Black.

## BOBBY CLARKE TRIVIA

9. How many times did Bobby Clarke record over 100 points in a season?
A. 5.          B. 4          C. 3          D. 2

10. Bobby Clarke's rookie season was 1969-70. How many goals did he score that year?
A. 12          B. 23          C. 15.          D. 26

11. At the time Bobby Clarke retired in 1984, what was his standing in NHL history for career assists?
A. 4th          B. 5th          C. 2nd          D. 8th

12. Which of the following teams did Bobby Clarke not serve as General Manager?
A. Toronto Maple Leafs     B. Florida Panthers
C. Philadelphia Flyers     D. Minnesota North Stars

13. Which of the following awards did Bobby Clarke not win?
A. Hart Trophy          B. Masterson Trophy
C. Selke Trophy          D. Conn Smythe Trophy

14. Who succeeded Bobby Clarke as captain of the Flyers after the 1978-79 season?
A. Darryl Sittler          B. Bill Barber
C. Mel Bridgman          D. Rick MacLeish

15. Who succeeded Bobby Clarke as captain of the Flyers upon his retirement in 1984?
A. Rick Tocchet          B. Mark Howe
C. Bill Barber          D. Dave Poulin

16. Who did Bobby Clarke succeed as captain at the start of the 1972-73 season?
A. Lou Angotti          B. Ed Van Impe
C. Larry Zeidel          D. Gerry Meehan

143

**answers on page 180**

# FLYER'D UP!

Trivia, Facts, and Anecdotes for Fans of the Orange and Black.

## BOBBY CLARKE TRIVIA

17. Bobby Clarke wore two jersey numbers during his career. One was 16 – which was the other?

A. 26.            B. 36            C. 6.            D. 9

18. Bobby Clarke was named General Manager of the Flyers in 1984. Whom did he succeed?

A. Bob McCammon            B. Pat Quinn
C. Keith Allen            D. Jay Snider

19. During the 1972 Summit Series while playing for Team Canada, Bobby Clarke slashed which member of the Soviet Union on the ankle?

A. Valeri Kharlamov            B. Vitaly Davydov
C. Boris Mikailov            D. Vladimir Petrov

20. Bobby Clarke was selected by the Flyers in the second round (17th overall in the 1969 NHL draft). Who did the Flyers select in the first round?

A. Lew Morrison            B. Serge Bernier
C. Al Sarault            D. Bob Currier

21. Bobby Clarke was born in what Canadian town and province?

A) Medicine Hat, Alberta            B) Flin Flon, Manitoba
C) Thunder Bay, Ontario            D) Toronto, Ontario

22. Which Flyers General manager selected Bobby Clarke in the 1969 NHL Amatuer Draft?

A) Gerry Melnyk            B) Keith Allen
C) Bud Polie            D) Ed Snider

23. Bobby Clarke's first point in the NHL came October 22,1969 against which NHL Team?

A) Chicago Black Hawks            B) Minnesota North Stars
C) Toronto Maple Leafs            D) Montreal Canadiens

**answers on page 180**

# FLYER'D UP!

Trivia, Facts, and Anecdotes for Fans of the Orange and Black.

# WHAT IF...

*There is a time in the life of every Flyer fan when he sits around a bar, sips a cold beverage and thinks about the past. He thinks about all the remarkable games, amazing goals, spectacular saves and incredible playoff runs. Then come the agonizing losses; along with the associated sentiment and suffering comes the "what ifs". It's simple to change history in the mind and fantasize about how things could have turned out differently. I have had conversations with fans, former players, members of the organization, and countless colleagues; the result: the following compellation of the biggest "what ifs" in Flyers' history. When reading the list, take a moment to ponder how things could've turned out.*

### What if the Eric Lindros trade with Quebec never happened?

While the Flyers were rebuilding, the thought process was to trade in order to acquire a true superstar. Although the deal with Quebec in June of 1992 took time to materialize, it eventually awarded Eric Lindros to the Flyers. With their new star at the helm, the Flyers went on to three Eastern Conference Finals and appeared to fight for the Stanley Cup in 1997. It was a run that consisted of entertaining and exciting moments, which ushered in a new era of Flyers' hockey.

Unfortunately for the organization and its fans, they never won the Cup with the Lindros; to make matters worse, the momentum the team created quickly dissipated due to the deteriorating relationship between the Lindros

# FLYER'D UP!

Trivia, Facts, and Anecdotes for Fans of the Orange and Black.

family and the organization. The feud between Flyers' General Manager Bob Clarke and "Team Lindros" was the most dysfunctional relationship the organization has ever had with one of its players.

So, what if the Flyers never traded for Lindros? Would Peter Forsberg and Mike Ricci have led the team to the Promised Land? Who would be alongside them? Would the New York Rangers have won the Stanley Cup in 1994 if they had traded away John Vanbiesbrouck, James Patrick and others? Would the Quebec Nordiques have had a successful relocation to Colorado without the trade that netted them Peter Forsberg and Patrick Roy down the line?

What if the Flyers had indeed gone through with the trade but substituted the popular Rod Brind'Amour instead of the young Mike Ricci? They may have then been able to send out a line up with both Lindros and Peter Forsberg. The trade had more delineations than even the most difficult mathematical equations but, even though the team never won the Cup, the Lindros era of awe-inspiring hockey was worth the eventual question marks.

### What if the Flyers had successfully signed the Stastny Brothers from the Czechoslovakian National Team during the late 70's?

If the Flyers had successfully signed the pair, the top three lines would have been an offensive explosion. The famed "LCB line" of Reggie Leach, Bobby Clarke and Bill Barber would be followed by a second line of Peter, Marian and Anton Stastny; the third line would be some combination of Rick MacLeish, Mel Bridgman, Ken Linseman, and Brian Propp. The team would have been particularly tough to shut down -- Peter Stastny alone

**What If...**

*Did you know that after the Flyers last won the Stanley Cup in 1975, they lost their next 5 appearances in the finals to teams that went on to win multiple cups? (Lost to Montreal in 76, Montreal went on to win 3 straight, lost to New York Islanders in 1980, New York went on to win 3 straight, lost to Edmonton Oilers in 1985 and 1987, Edmonton won cups in 88 and 90 and finally lost to Detroit in 1997 where Detroit went on to repeat in 98 versus Washington.)*

# FLYER'D UP!

Trivia, Facts, and Anecdotes for Fans of the Orange and Black.

scored 450 goals and added 789 assists for a total of 1239 points in his career during regular season. He was one of only seven players in NHL history to record at least six consecutive seasons with over 100 points. What could've been!

## What if Bernie Parent had never been traded to Toronto in January of 1971?

The Flyers did obtain Rick MacLeish in the three-way trade, but the big story was how Parent blossomed into a great goalie under his boyhood hero, Jacques Plante. It was in Toronto that Parent mastered his craft, became technically sound and gained valuable experience. There, he succeeded in having the "double hat trick" of Stanley Cups and Vezina and Conn Smythe Trophies.

## What if Tim Kerr were healthy in the 1987 Finals versus the Edmonton Oilers?

In one of the greatest seven game series in the history of the NHL, the Flyers, who had come back from a three games to one deficit, fell valiantly at the Northlands Coliseum at Edmonton. Not only were the Flyers playing in their 26th playoff contest, but they were also without Tim Kerr, who tallied 58 goals that season. Kerr was one of many Flyers who were injured or out. He may have been enough to swing Game 7, which was a one-goal game until the final minutes. I'll spare defenseman Doug Crossman for missing a wide open net in the early minutes of Game 7 and blame the heart wrenching loss on the injuries. Oh, what if!

# FLYER'D UP!

Trivia, Facts, and Anecdotes for Fans of the Orange and Black.

## What if the Flyers had traded Rod Brind'Amour for Brendan Shanahan for the 1996-97 season?

Shanahan was a productive goal scorer who was headed toward great things (which was in the opposite direction of the Hartford Whalers' organization). He wanted a trade and many believed that the Flyers would be a perfect fit. After playing in just two games for the Whalers, he was sent to Detroit where he helped the Red Wings win the Stanley Cup against (you guessed it) the Flyers. It was Detroit's first Cup in 42 seasons; the Flyers were again denied a third parade down Broad Street. Looking back, I don't think they'd have won the Cup, even with Shanahan. Goaltending and defense were the main problem and the reason they were swept.

## What if linesman Leon Stickle hadn't blown the offside call in Game 6 of the 1980 Finals versus the New York Islanders?

The 1980 Flyers squad was one of the most balanced teams the Flyers have ever put on the ice. While the Flyers were tired and injured and the Islanders power play was clicking at a scary and ungodly percentage, the Flyers still could have forced a Game 7. The Islanders probably would have had the ultimate advantage in the series, but "what if" still runs through my mind. Who knows for sure what the result would have been, but I would have loved to have seen it.

## What if the Bruins' Bobby Orr hadn't been called for a penalty late in Game 6 of the 1974 Finals?

On May 19th, 1974, the Boston Bruins were attacking on Spectrum ice late in the third period of Game 6. The Flyers clung to a 1-0 lead. With just

# FLYER'D UP!

Trivia, Facts, and Anecdotes for Fans of the Orange and Black.

2:22 remaining, the legendary Bruins defenseman Bobby Orr was whistled for holding by referee Art Skov for grabbing Bobby Clarke on a sure to be a breakaway. The Flyers killed the penalty and went on to win the 1974 Stanley Cup. If Orr hadn't been in the box for the game's last two minutes, even Bernie Parent may not have been able to preserve the 1-0 lead the rest of the way. We'll take it.

## *What if Pelle Lindbergh hadn't died in a horrific car crash in November of 1985?*

Would the Flyers had gone on to win the Stanley Cup with Lindbergh between the pipes? Or would Ron Hextall have beaten him out in the coming years? Furthermore, would Lindbergh had been so entrenched in the position that Hextall would have never gotten a shot to play for the Flyers? Following the Lindbergh tragedy, the Flyers lost in the first round of the playoffs in five games to the New York Rangers. The season left many shaking their heads of what could've been if the loveable Swede had still been around. According to Full Spectrum author Jay Greenberg, in the hours after Lindbergh's death, head coach Mike Keenan sat on the floor of his office mourning the loss and uttered, "There goes the Stanley Cup." Keenan knew the Flyers lost more much more than that, though -- they lost a member of their own family.

# FLYER'D UP!

Trivia, Facts, and Anecdotes for Fans of the Orange and Black.

## TROPHIES AND AWARDS TRIVIA

1. The Barry Ashee Trophy was first awarded to whom?
A. Joe Watson
B. Jimmy Watson
C. Andre Dupont
D. Bob Dailey

2. The first member of the Flyers organization inducted into the NHL Hall of Fame was:
A. Bobby Clarke
B. Keith Allen
C. Bernie Parent
D. Ed Snider

3. The Pelle Lindbergh Memorial Trophy is awarded to the Flyer who is:
A. MVP
B. Most Improved
C. Class Guy
D. Best Goaltender

4. The Bobby Clarke Trophy was first awarded to whom?
A. Pelle Lindbergh
B. Ron Hextall
C. Mark Howe
D. Dave Poulin

5. The Bobby Clarke Trophy is awarded to the Flyer who is:
A. Most Improved
B. MVP
C. Class Guy
D. Best Defenseman

6. Who was awarded the first-ever Barry Ashbee Award?
A. Don Nachbaur
B. Mike Stothers
C. Tim Tookey
D. Al Hill

7. Who was the first-ever repeat winner of the Barry Ashbee Trophy?
A. Jimmy Watson
B. Joe Watson
C. Mark Howe
D. Eric Desjardins

8 The Yanick Dupre Class Guy Memorial Award was first won by whom?
A. Eric Desjardins
B. Keith Jones
C. Trent Klatt
D. Keith Primeau

9. All of the following have won the Bobby Clarke Trophy more than once EXCEPT:
A. Eric Lindros
B. Mark Recchi
C. Ron Hextall
D. Rod Brind'Amour

150

**answers on page 181**

# FLYER'D UP!

Trivia, Facts, and Anecdotes for Fans of the Orange and Black.

## TROPHIES AND AWARDS TRIVIA

10. All of the following Flyers have won the Vezina Trophy as the NHL's best goaltender EXCEPT:
A. Bernie Parent
B. Bob Froese
C. Pelle Lindbergh
D. Ron Hextall

11. Which trophy did Tim Kerr win in 1989?
A. Bill Masterton Memorial Trophy
B. Lady Bing Award
C. Lester Patrick Trophy
D. Bud Ice Plus/Minus Award

12. All of the following won the Jack Adams Award for the NHL Coach of the Year EXCEPT:
A. Bill Barber
B. Patt Quinn
C. Fred Shero
D. John Stevens

13. Eric Lindros did not win the 1995 Art Ross Trophy as the NHL's leading scorer due to a tiebreaking loss to which other player?
A. Steve Yzerman
B. Joe Sakic
C. Wayne Gretzky
D. Jaromir Jagr

14. Dave Poulin won which major trophy for the 1986-87 season?
A. Lester B. Pearson Award
B. Frank J. Selke Trophy
C. Lady Bing
D. Bill Masterton Memorial Trophy

15. All of the following Flyers won the William M. Jennings Trophy EXCEPT:
A. Roman Cechmanek
B. Robert Esche
C. Bob Froese
D. John Vanbiesbrouck

16. The last Flyer to win the Hart Trophy as NHL MVP was:
A. Eric Lindros
B. John LeClair
C. Peter Forsberg
D. Bobby Clarke

17. Eric Desjardins won the Barry Ashbee Trophy six consecutive times from 1995 to 2000. Which Flyer won the Trophy in 1994?
A. Steve Duchesne
B. Kjell Samuelson
C. Garry Galley
D. Gord Murphy

answers on page 181

# FLYER'D UP!

Trivia, Facts, and Anecdotes for Fans of the Orange and Black.

## TROPHIES AND AWARDS TRIVIA

18. All of the following Flyers won the Conn Smythe Trophy EXCEPT:
A. Reggie Leach          B. Pelle Lindbergh
C. Bernie Parent         D. Ron Hextall

19. The only Flyer ever to win the Emery Edge Award was:
A. Mark Howe             B. Brad McCrimmon
C. Paul Coffey           D. Joe Watson

20. Who were the first non-players to be inducted into the Flyers' Hall of Fame?
A. Fred Shero and Keith Allen      B. Keith Allen and Ed Snider
C. Ed Snider and Joe Scott         D. Gene Hart and Keith Allen

21. Who was the first Flyer recipient of the Toyota Cup?
A. Simon Gagne           B. Keith Primeau
C. Roman Cechmanek       D. Mark Recchi

22. All of the following numbers are retired by the Flyers EXCEPT:
A. 31          B. 7          C. 16          D. 4

23. Which trophy has a member of the Flyers never been awarded?
A. Lady Bing             B. Norris Trophy
C. Calder Trophy         D. All of the above

24. Who are the only two Flyers to have won the Frank J. Selke Trophy?
A. Bobby Clarke and Dave Poulin        B. Dave Poulin and Keith Primeau
C. Bobby Clarke and Rod Brind'Amour    D. Dave Poulin and Brian Propp

25. How many times did Eric Lindros win the Bobby Clarke Trophy?
A. 6          B. 5.          C. 3          D. 4

26. All of the following goaltenders have won the Bobby Clarke Trophy except for:
A) Pelle Lindbergh        B) Ron Hextall
C) Pete Peeters           D) Roman Cechmanek

152

# FLYER'D UP!

Trivia, Facts, and Anecdotes for Fans of the Orange and Black.

# 7 Great Trades in Flyers History

*7. Flyers trade Alexei Zhitnik to Atlanta Thrashers for Braydon Coburn.*
*February 24, 2007*

This trade at first was thought to have taken a few years to pan out but Flyers General Manager Paul Holmgren looks to be declared the flat out winner in this one, fleecing Thrashers General Manager Don Waddell in a foundation setting move.

Coburn was drafted by the Thrashers in the first round (eighth overall) of the 2003 NHL Entry Draft and had tremendous upside at the time of the deal. Holmgren told reporters after the trade was made that he was very pleased to acquire Coburn. He should've been.

"Braydon is a player who we have liked since his draft year," offered Holmgren."He is a big, young defenseman that skates very well. He will fit in nicely with our young group."

And he has, solidifying himself as a top four defenseman for the Flyers, flourishing under the guidance of veteran Kimmo Timonen. Coburn should be a fixture along the Flyers blue line for years to come.

As for Zhitnik, the journeyman defenseman whom the Flyers acquired in 2006 from the New York Islanders is no longer in the NHL and played just

# FLYER'D UP!

Trivia, Facts, and Anecdotes for Fans of the Orange and Black.

83 games for the Thrashers before moving back to his native Russia following the 2007-08 season.

### *6. Flyers trade Ron Sutter and Murray Baron to St. Louis Blues for Rod Brind'Amour and Dan Quinn.*
*September 22, 1991*

Ron Sutter gave 8 plus solid seasons for the Flyers, playing in two Stanley Cup Finals and was widely considered one of the team's top defensive forwards while also adding a scoring punch. Sutter was thought of as the consummate Flyer. However, the Flyers had begun rebuilding in the early 1990's and the veteran center was shipped to the Blues, along with Murray Baron in exchange for who would turn out to become one of the most popular players in franchise history in Rod Brind'Amour.

Brind'Amour gave the Flyers 8 professional seasons, proving to be a true leader, a great shut down center, and one of the most durable players to have ever worn the orange and black. Brind'Amour registered 601 points for the Flyers in 633 regular season contests and currently stands ninth all time in Flyers history. Brind'Amour's incredible work ethic allowed him to play in a franchise record 484 consecutive games, playing a major role in the team's resurgence in the mid 1990's.

Brind'Amour was eventually traded to the Carolina Hurricanes during the 1999-2000 for Keith Primeau, where he went on to win a Stanley Cup, serving as the Hurricanes Captain in 2006.

# FLYER'D UP!

Trivia, Facts, and Anecdotes for Fans of the Orange and Black.

Oh, and Dan Quinn? Although he had a decent career in the NHL, averaging just under a point per game (.85) during his 14 seasons, he was surely not the centerpiece in this deal. It was all about Rod Brind'Amour.

*Upshall*

***5. Flyers trade Peter Forsberg to Nashville Predators for Ryan Parent, Scottie Upshall, 2007 1st Rounder (later transferred back to Nashville-Jonathon Blum) & 2007 3rd Rounder (transferred to Washington-Phil Desimone). First rounder was eventually traded to Nashville for the rights to Scott Hartnell and Kimmo Timonen.***
*February 15, 2007 and*
*June 18, 2007*

*Hartnell*

Not since the Eric Lindros trade with the Quebec Nordiques in June of 92 did the landscape of the Flyers roster change so quickly. This deal was yet another indication that General Manager Paul Holmgren indeed had a plan for quickly refurbishing and redesigning a hockey club that suffered its worst season in its illustrious history during the in 2006-007.

*Timonen*

In February of 2007, it was becoming abundantly clear that Flyers were going to miss the post season and correctly started to field offers from many clubs inquiring about the rights to Peter Forsberg. Forsberg, unsure about his health due to chronic problems with is right ankle apparently was unsure about his future as well. His lack of commitment to sign a new contract in Philadelphia all but forced the Flyers to move their former first round draft pick, or risk losing him for nothing.

# FLYER'D UP!

Trivia, Facts, and Anecdotes for Fans of the Orange and Black.

In two dynamic moves with the Nashville Predators, Holmgren was able to move the one-time but ailing NHL great for a spark plug forward in Scottie Upshall, a terrific defensive prospect in Ryan Parent and the Predators first round selection in 2007 and then 6 months later deftly send the aforementioned draft pick back to Nashville for the exclusive negotiating rights to free agents Scott Hartnell and Kimmo Timonen. The Flyers signed both to long-term deals.

While Upshall, Hartnell and especially Timonen, the Flyers best defenseman, have paid huge dividends to their club, the same can't be said for Forsberg and his impact in Nashville.

All four players that have come Philadelphia's direction as a result of these two dealings with Nashville played a role in the team's dramatic turnaround during the 2007-2008 season, of which the Flyers fell just three games shy of reaching the Stanley Cup Final, and are integral components of their current roster in 2009.

As for Forsberg, he played in just 17 regular season games for the Predators and failed to lead them to the Stanley Cup Finals. Forsberg's Predators were eliminated by the San Jose Sharks in 5 games with Forsberg notching just 4 points in the series.

### 4. Flyers trade 1973 First Rounder (Bob Neely) and future considerations (Doug Favell) to Toronto Maple Leafs for the rights to Bernie Parent and 1973 Second Rounder (Larry Goodenough)
*May 15, 1973*

In January of 1971, the Flyers made the foolish mistake of trading Bernie Parent to the Toronto Maple Leafs in their search for more offensive pro-

# FLYER'D UP!

Trivia, Facts, and Anecdotes for Fans of the Orange and Black.

duction. In May of 1973, they rectified their error, and witnessed the greatest goaltender in the history of their organization lead them to consecutive Stanley Cups.

Bernie Parent was chosen in the 1967 expansion draft by the Flyers and preceded to play 4 seasons with the orange and black. Unexplainably, in the winter of 1971, the Flyers were searching for more offense and traded the promising goaltender to the Toronto Maple Leafs along with a second rounder (Rick Kehoe) for Mike Walton, Bruce Gamble and a 1971 first rounder (Pierre Plante). Sadly, the only player besides Parent in this deal that had a notable career in the NHL was Kehoe, who went on to record 767 points, most as a member of the Pittsburgh Penguins. Plante did go onto to marginal success, playing in 599 NHL contests.

As for Parent, he spent two seasons back with the Maple Leafs in 72 and 73, where he blossomed under the tutelage of future Hall of Famer Jacques Plante. Then in the spring of 73, in a twist of fate and serendipity for the Flyers, Parent's rights were traded back to the Flyers, after a contract dispute with the Leafs left him laboring in the WHA. He was once again a member of the Flyers. And the rest is history. Glorious history.

Parent would be the backbone of the Flyers success, leading the team to Stanley Cups in 1974 and 1975, winning back-to-back Vezina and Conn Smythe trophies in the process. Parent retired from the Flyers in 1979 and was inducted into the NHL Hall of Fame in 1984. Thank you Toronto.

# FLYER'D UP!

Trivia, Facts, and Anecdotes for Fans of the Orange and Black.

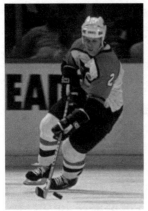

***3. Flyers trade Greg Adams, Ken Linesman, 1983 first rounder (David Jensen) and 1983 third rounder (Leif Karlsson) to Hartford Whalers for Mark Howe and a 1983 third rounder (Derrick Smith)***
*August 20, 1982*

It isn't every day that a team is able to acquire not only a player possessing the sport's greatest DNA, but one with the pure natural ability and gifts to become one of the greatest players in franchise history. Yet, inconceivably, on a steamy summer day in 1982, Flyers General Manager Keith Allen was able to pry Mark Howe away from the Hartford Whalers and into the orange and black. Not a bad days work.

Howe, of course, the son of the then greatest player in NHL history, Gordie Howe was a tremendously talented defenseman playing for the new Hartford Whalers but in 1981 had suffered a near career ending injury in a collision, sliding into the then immoveable nets. The injury was so severe, that the Whalers went in to conservation mode, trading Howe to the Flyers for 4 players, most notably Ken Linesman.

Let me be the first to say, I enjoyed watching The Rat play, and at the time of the trade, I was deeply saddened that the Flyers no longer would have Linesman, and his fiesty play in the line-up. I, as well as Philadelphia, got over that loss in a hurry.

Howe would go on to a legendary career in Philadelphia. His effortless, skating style and offensive flair were the perfect complement with his long time defense partner Brad McCrimmon. Howe backboned the Flyers blue

# FLYER'D UP!

Trivia, Facts, and Anecdotes for Fans of the Orange and Black.

line during their cup runs of the mid eighties as he played 10 seasons in Philadelphia, and his 480 points are still today, tops in Flyers history amongst defenseman.

As for the other notable components in the deal. Linesman went on to play 10 more productive seasons in the NHL, mostly as a member of the Edmonton Oilers and Boston Bruins, and a brief return to the Flyers during the 1990 season after a deal involving popular Dave Poulin.

We shouldn't forget either, the "throw in" draft pick the Whalers sent the Flyers way. The Flyers used that pick in 1983 to select Derrick Smith, who spent seven seasons with the Flyers from 1984-1991.

## 2. Flyers trade Larry Wright, Al MacAdam & 1974 1st Rounder (Ron Chipperfield) to California Golden Seals for Reggie Leach.
*May 24, 1974*

The Flyers were just Stanley Cup Champions for 5 days but General Manager Keith Allen knew that his team would need more of an offensive scoring punch if they were going to repeat as champions of the NHL. Allen coveted immediate, proven scoring help and landed it when he acquired Reggie Leach.

Reggie "The Rifle" Leach was coming off three productive seasons in the NHL as a member of the Boston Bruins and California Golden Seals. Leach, in just 171 professional games, recorded 58 goals and 114 points and was showing the offensive flair that made the Bruins select him third overall in the 1970 Amateur Draft. To acquire him however, the Flyers thought they had to pay a serious price.

# FLYER'D UP!

Trivia, Facts, and Anecdotes for Fans of the Orange and Black.

The Flyers traded, along with a 1974 first round draft choice (Ron Chipperfield), Larry Wright, their former first round draft pick, (8th overall) in the 1971 draft. Wright was a tremendous prospect but it was clear that by judging from his 36 games with the Flyers, the center would need more seasoning to be an effective NHL player. Wright registered just 2 points, both assists.

The other key to the deal for California was right-winger Al MacAdam. MacAdam was also a former draft choice of the Flyers, whom they selected in the 4th round of the 1972 Amateur Draft. MacAdam played in just 5 games for the Flyers and although he had tremendous upside, the Flyers were looking to remain among the elite in the NHL, and decided to include him in the deal.

A future first round draft choice, a former first round draft selection and a promising right wing seemed like an awful lot to give up for Leach, but Allen made the deal, and as history showed, he made the right decision.

Leach went on to be a blazing success with the Flyers. For the next 8 seasons, Leach scored 306 goals, including a still Flyers record 61 during the 1975-76 season. During the 1976 NHL Playoffs, Leach scored a record 19 playoff goals and still remains the only non-goaltender to win the award in a losing cause. The Flyers were swept by Montreal 4-0.

Leach ranks 11th all time in Flyers scoring with 514 points and was inducted into the Flyers Hall of Fame in 1992.

California wasn't totally fleeced on the deal. They missed on Wright and Chipperfield. Wright never panned and in fact ended back with the Flyers for two games in the 1975-76 season but his career was mostly spent toiling

# FLYER'D UP!

Trivia, Facts, and Anecdotes for Fans of the Orange and Black.

in the minor leagues. As for Chipperfield, he had a productive WHA career and spent 83 games in the NHL, but none for the Seals.

They did get it right with MacAdam however. MacAdam ended up playing 11 more seasons in the NHL, 10 of which were played with the California/Cleveland/ Minnesota franchise. He spent his last season in the NHL with Vancouver but did retire with a respectable 591 points in 864 NHL games.

MacAdam may have scored more points in his NHL career than Leach did with the Flyers, but the natural goal scoring ability of Leach placed together with hall of famers Bobby Clarke and Bill Barber on the famed LCB line made the trade worth its weight in gold, and silver!

## *1. Flyers trade Mark Recchi & 1995 3rd Rounder (Martin Hohenberger) to Montreal Canadiens for Eric Desjardins, John LeClair, and Gilbert Dionne*
*February 9, 1995*

There hasn't been a bigger theft since the Lufthansa Heist at John F. Kennedy Airport in December of 78.

Flyers General Manager Bob Clarke made a lot of shrewd moves over the years but the deal he made on a cold February night not only accomplished its goal of shaking the team from its doldrums, but it changed Flyers history forever. The results from this trade did not produce a Stanley Cup but

# FLYER'D UP!

Trivia, Facts, and Anecdotes for Fans of the Orange and Black.

it can be argued that acquiring future Flyers greats Eric Desjardins and John LeClair eventually restored the franchise's elite status in the NHL and it was the perfect complement to the team's franchise player Eric Lindros.

Recchi was a very popular Flyer and a productive one as well. After all, Recchi was brought to Philadelphia in exchange for another fan favorite in Rick Tocchet in 1992. For the next three seasons, Recchi was an offensive force, jelling with Lindros and Brent Fedyk to create the Crazy Eights line.

Recchi produced a 123-point season in the 92-93 season, which still stands today as the Flyers single season record.

Still, Clarke coveted a scoring winger to complement Lindros and had his sights on a number one, puck carrying defenseman. How he got the Canadiens General Manager Serge Savard to give him all that he desired in one deal was either pure genius or a stroke of luck. Either way, the Flyers got the best of this deal from the start, and even ended up re-acquiring Recchi in the 1998-99 season.

As for LeClair and Desjardins, they became part of the Flyers family and will be regarded throughout time as two of the greatest Flyers in club history.

LeClair, who came to Flyers already a Stanley Cup winner in Montreal, became a fan favorite and was the missing piece to what was to become the Legion of Doom, the most dominating line in hockey, joining Lindros and Swede Mikael Renberg.

# FLYER'D UP!

Trivia, Facts, and Anecdotes for Fans of the Orange and Black.

In 1998, LeClair became the first American-born NHL player to record three consecutive 50-goal seasons and the second Flyer to do so, behind Tim Kerr. LeClair played for the Flyers for 10 seasons and was one of the most productive players in franchise history, scoring 382 career goals and an additional 42 in the playoffs, statistics good enough for the top 10 in the history of Flyers goal scorers. With Lindros and LeClair in place, the Flyers knocked on the precipice of Stanley Cup glory, getting the closest in 1997 but ultimately getting swept by Detroit in the finals.

Desjardins also went on to accomplish great things as a Flyer, and is now considered and talked about in the same breath as Howe as perhaps the greatest defenseman in Flyers history.

Desjardins was the clearly the center piece of this deal, already an All-Star and Stanley Cup winner, he instantly brought to stability to the Flyers blue line and made those around him better.

Desjardins went on to win 7 Barry Ashbee Trophies as the team's top defender and compiled 396 points, second only to Howe in Flyers lore.

There is no doubt that both players acquired in this legendary deal, perhaps Recchi as well, will be one day enshrined into the Flyers Hall of Fame. Gilbert Dionne won't.

# FLYER'D UP!

Trivia, Facts, and Anecdotes for Fans of the Orange and Black.

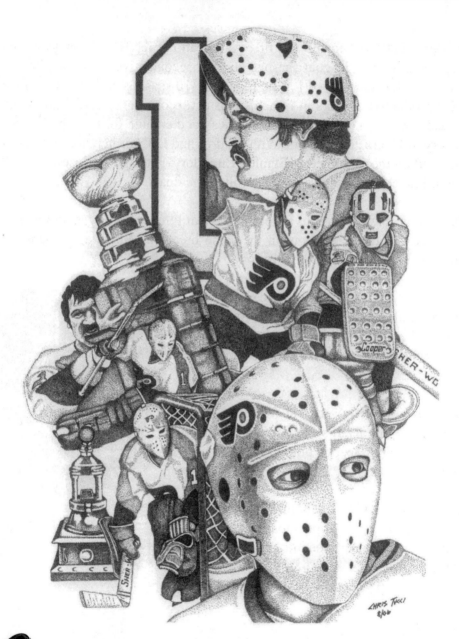

# FLYER'D UP!

Trivia, Facts, and Anecdotes for Fans of the Orange and Black.

## BRIAN'S LIST OF BEST
## PHILADELPHIA FLYERS A TO Z

**A**...Barry Ashbee

**B**... Bill Barber

**C**...Bob Clarke

**D**...Eric Desjardins

**E**...Pelle Eklund

**F**...Peter Forsberg

**G**...Simon Gagne

**H**...Mark Howe

**I**...Gary Innes (by default)

**J**...Kim Johnsson

**K**...Tim Kerr

**L**...Eric Lindros

**M**...Rick MacLeish

**N**...Simon Nolet

**O**...Joel Otto

**P**...Bernie Parent

**Q**...Dan Quinn (by default)

**R**...Marc Recchi

**S**...Dave Schultz

**T**...Rick Tocchet

**U**...R. J. Umberger

**V**...Ed Van Impe

**W**...Joe Watson

**X**...None

**Y**...Dmitry Yuskevich

**Z**...Peter Zezel

# FLYERS ALL-TIME ROSTER 1967-2008

| NO. | POS. | PLAYER | SEASON (S) |
|---|---|---|---|
| 25 | C | ACTON, Keith | 1988-93 |
| 36, 25 | LW | ADAMS, Greg | 1980-82 |
| 27 | LW | Afanasenkov, Dmitry | 2006-07 |
| 19, 36 | RW | ALLISON, Ray | 1981-85, 86-87 |
| 11 | RW | AMONTE, Tony | 2002-04 |
| 37 | D | ANDERSON, Shawn | 1994-95 |
| 14 | LW | ANDERSSON, Mikael | 1998-00 |
| 7 | C | ANGOTTI, Lou | 1967-68 |
| 8 | LW | ANTOSKI, Shawn | 1994-96 |
| 58 | LW | ARMSTRONG, Bill H. | 1990-92 |
| 6 | D | ARTHUR, Fred | 1981-82 |
| 4 | D | ASHBEE, Barry | 1970-74 |
| | | | |
| 44 | D | BABYCH, Dave | 1997-99 |
| 34, 35, 36, 9 | D | BAILEY, Reid | 1980-82 |
| 24 | D | BALL, Terry | 1967-68, 69-70 |
| 7 | LW | BARBER, Bill | 1972-85 |
| 23, 25 | D | BARNES, Norm | 1976-77, 79-81 |
| 8 | D | BARON, Murray | 1989-91 |
| 20, 34 | RW | BARRIE, Len | 1990-93 |
| 32 | D | BAST, Ryan | 1998-00 |
| 21, 31, 5 | D | BATHE, Frank | 1977-84 |
| 5 | D | BAUMGARTNER, Nolan | 2006-07 |
| 35 | G | BEAUREGARD. Stephane | 1992-93 |
| 30, 35 | G | BELHUMEUR, Michel | 1972-73 |
| 22 | LW | BENNETT, Harvey | 1976-78 |
| 19 | D | BENNING, Brian | 1991-93 |
| 42 | LW | BERANEK, Josef | 1992-95 |
| 19, 42 | C | BERGEN, Todd | 1984-85 |
| 37, 19 | C | BERGLUND, Bo | 1985-86 |
| 19, 21 | C | BERNIER, Serge | 1968-72 |
| 34, 17, 12, 32 | LW | BERUBE, Craig | 1986-91, 98-00 |
| 46 | C | BIGGS, Don | 1989-90 |
| 43 | G | BIRON, Martin | 2006-** |
| 8 | LW | BLACKBURN, Don | 1967-69 |
| 4, 23, 3 | D | BLADON, Tom | 1972-78 |
| 33 | | BLOSKI, Mike (DNP) | 1985-86 |
| 40, 10 | LW | BOIVIN, Claude | 1991-94 |
| 17, 5 | RW | BOLAND, Mike A. | 1974-75 |
| 28 | D | BOTELL, Mark | 1981-82 |
| 33 | G | BOUCHER, Brian | 1999-02 |
| 21, 36 | RW | BOULERICE, Jesse | 2001-02, 2007-08 |
| 28, 53, 8, 34 | D | BOWEN, Jason | 1992-97 |
| 87 | LW | BRASHEAR, Donald | 2001-06 |
| 55 | RW | BRENDL, Pavel | 2001-03 |
| 34 | LW | BRICKLEY, Andy | 1982-83 |
| 10 | C | BRIDGMAN, Mel | 1975-82 |
| 48 | C | BRIERE, Danny | 2007-** |
| 40, 3 | D | BRIMANIS, Aris | 1993-94, 95-97 |
| 17 | C/LW | BRIND'AMOUR, Rod | 1991-00 |

*Bill Barber*

| NO. | POS. | PLAYER | SEASON (S) |
|---|---|---|---|
| 25, 3, 10 | D | BROSSART, Willie | 1970-73 |
| 32, 21 | RW | BROWN, Dave | 1982-89, 91-95 |
| 3 | D | BROWN, Larry | 1971-72 |
| 10 | C | BULLARD, Mike | 1988-90 |
| 28 | C | BUREAU, Marc | 1998-00 |
| 33, 41 | G | BURKE, Sean | 1997-98, 2003-04 |
| 2 | D | BURT, Adam | 1998-00 |
| 21, 28 | D | BUSNIUK, Mike | 1979-81 |
| 22, 26 | C | BUTSAYEV, Viacheslav | 1992-94 |
| 22 | RW | BYERS, Mike | 1968-69 |

*Dave Brown*

| NO. | POS. | PLAYER | SEASON (S) |
|---|---|---|---|
| 19 | LW | CALDER, Kyle | 2006-07 |
| 28 | RW | CALLANDER, Drew | 1976-79 |
| 29 | D | CARKNER, Terry | 1988-93 |
| 21 | D | CARRUTHERS, Dwight | 1967-68 |
| 18 | LW | CARSON, Lindsay | 1981-88 |
| 17 | C | CARTER, Jeff | 2005-** |
| 32 | G | CECHMANEK, Roman | 2000-03 |
| 35 | G | CHABOT, Frederic | 1993-94 |
| 5 | D | CHERRY, Dick | 1968-70 |
| 19, 15 | RW | ChouinArd, Eric | 2002-04, 05-06 |
| 40, 6 | D | CHYCHRUN, Jeff | 1986-91 |
| 36, 16 | C | CLARKE, Bobby | 1969-84 |
| 15, 10 | C | CLEMENT, Bill | 1971-75 |
| 5 | D | COBURN, Braydon | 2006-** |
| 44, 9, 35, 29 | D/LW | COCHRANE, Glen | 1978-79, 81-84 |
| 77 | D | Coffey, Paul | 1996-98 |
| 23 | RW | COLLINS, Bill | 1976-77 |
| 89 | C | COMRIE, Mike | 2003-04 |
| 46, 15 | RW | CONROY, Al | 1991-94 |
| 22 | C | Corkum, Bob | 1995-96 |
| 33, 32 | LW | COTE, Riley | 2006-** |
| 27 | LW | COWICK, Bruce | 1973-74 |
| 32 | LW/C | CRAVEN, Murray | 1984-91 |
| 29, 15 | C | CRISP, Terry | 1972-77 |
| 44 | D | CRONIN, Shawn | 1992-93 |
| 3 | D | CROSSMAN, Doug | 1983-88 |
| 26 | RW | CROWE, Phil | 1995-96 |
| 14 | C | CULLEN, Matt | 2006-07 |
| 12 | RW | CUMMINS, Jim | 1993-94 |
| 21 | C | CUNNINGHAM, Jimmy | 1977-78 |
| | | | |
| 19, 11 | LW | DAIGLE, Alexandre | 1997-99 |
| 15 | D | DAIGNEAULT, Jean-Jacques | 1986-88 |
| 2 | D | DAILEY, Bob | 1976-82 |
| 24 | C | DALLMAN, Rod | 1991-92 |
| 49 | G | D'AMOUR, Marc | 1988-89 |
| 46, 14 | RW | DANIELS, Kimbi | 1990-92 |

# FLYER'D UP!

Trivia, Facts, and Anecdotes for Fans of the Orange and Black.

# FLYERS ALL-TIME ROSTER 1967-2008

| NO. | POS. | PLAYER | SEASON (S) |
|---|---|---|---|
| 8, 22 | LW | DANIELS, Scott | 1996-97 |
| 11, 14 | C | DARBY, Craig | 1996-98 |
| 29 | LW | DEAN, Barry | 1977-79 |
| 43 | D | DELMORE, Andy | 1998-01 |
| 37 | D | DESJARDINS, Eric | 1994-06 |
| 20, 9 | RW | DiMAIO, Rob | 1993-96 |
| 15 | RW | DIMITRAKOS, Niko | 2005-07 |
| 20, 11 | RW | DINEEN, Kevin | 1991-96 |
| 45 | LW | DIONNE, Gilbert | 1994-96 |

*Paul Coffey*

| NO. | POS. | PLAYER | SEASON (S) |
|---|---|---|---|
| 20 | RW | DIVISEK, Tomas | 2000-02 |
| 7, 18 | RW | DOBBIN, Brian | 1986-92 |
| 20 | C | DOPITA, Jiri | 2001-02 |
| 24, 12 | RW | DORNHOEFER, Gary | 1967-78 |
| 34 | C | DOWD, jim | 2007-08 |
| 27 | RW | DOWNIE, Steve | 2007-** |
| 23 | C | DROLET, Rene | 1971-72 |
| 26 | RW | DRUCE, John | 1995-98 |
| 19, 28, 25 | D | DUCHESNE, Steve | 1991-92, 98-99 |
| 32 | C | DUNLOP, Blake | 1977-79 |
| 28, 6 | D | DUPONT, Andre | 1972-80 |
| 66, 15, 18 | LW | DUPRE, Yanick | 1991-92, 94-96 |
| 9 | D | DVORAK, Miroslav | 1982-85 |
| 24, 29 | D | DYKHUIS, Karl | 1994-97, 98-00 |

| NO. | POS. | PLAYER | SEASON (S) |
|---|---|---|---|
| 55 | LW | EAGER, Ben | 2005-08 |
| 44 | D | EATON, Mark | 1999-00 |
| 21 | D | EDESTRAND, Darryl | 1969-70 |
| 9 | C | EKLUND, Pelle | 1985-94 |
| 23, 36 | RW | ELLISON, Matt | 2005-07 |
| 6, 8, 27 | D | ERIKSSON, Thomas | 1980-82, 83-86 |
| 42 | G | ESCHE, Robert | 2002-07 |
| 15 | C | EVANS, Doug | 1992-93 |
| 23, 25 | C | EVANS, John | 1978-79 80-81, 82-83 |

| NO. | POS. | PLAYER | SEASON (S) |
|---|---|---|---|
| 15 | RW | FALLOON, Pat | 1995-98 |
| 36 | LW | FAUST, Andre | 1992-94 |
| 1 | G | FAVELL, Doug | 1967-73 |
| 52, 29 | LW | FEDORUK, Todd | 2000-04, 06-07 |
| 26 | LW | FEDOTENKO, Ruslan | 2000-02 |
| 18 | RW | FEDYK, Brent | 1992-96 |
| 39 | D | FENYVES, Dave | 1987-92 |
| 25 | D | FINLEY, Jeff | 1993-94 |
| 7, 15 | C | FISHER, Craig | 1989-91 |
| 8 | D | Fitzpatrick, Rory | 2007-08 |
| 32, 22, 34, 39 | LW | FITZPATRICK, Ross | 1982-86 |
| 9 | LW | FLEMING, Reggie | 1969-70 |
| 21 | RW | FLETT, Bill | 1971-74 |

| NO. | POS. | PLAYER | SEASON (S) |
|---|---|---|---|
| 43, 11 | C | FLOCKHART, Ron | 1980-83 |
| 22 | D/LW | FOLEY, Rick | 1971-72 |
| 48, 12 | LW | Forbes, Colin | 1996-99 |
| 21 | C | FORSBERG, Peter | 2005-07 |
| 44 | D | FOSTER, Corey | 1991-92 |
| 35 | G | FOSTER, Norm (DNP) | 1993-94 |
| 29 | LW | FOTIU, Nick | 1987-88 |
| 45, 37 | C | FREER, Mark | 1986-92 |
| 35 | G | FROESE, Bob | 1982-87 |

| NO. | POS. | PLAYER | SEASON (S) |
|---|---|---|---|
| 12 | LW | GAGNE, Simon | 1999-** |
| 3 | D | GALLEY, Garry | 1991-95 |
| 30 | G | GAMBLE, Bruce | 1970-72 |
| 23 | C | GARDNER, Dave | 1979-80 |
| 23 | D | GAUTHIER, Denis | 2005-** |
| 5 | D | GAUTHIER, Jean | 1967-68 |
| 20, 11 | LW | GENDRON, Jean-Guy | 1968-72 |
| 21 | RW | GILLEN, Don | 1979-80 |
| 34 | LW | GILLIS, Jere | 1986-87 |
| 30 | | GILLOW, Russ (DNP) | 1971-72 |
| 49 | | GILMOUR, Darryl (DNP) | 1987-88 |
| 56 | RW | GIROUX, Claude | 2007-** |
| 4, 23, 5, 29 | D | GOODENOUGH, Larry | 1974-77 |
| 22, 36 | RW | GORENCE, Tom | 1978-83 |
| 52 | LW | GRANT, Tristen | 2006-** |
| 55, 77 | C | GRATTON, Chris | 1997-99 |
| 46 | LW | GRATTON, Josh | 2005-06 |
| 35 | G | GREENLAY, Mike (DNP) | 1994-95 |
| 65 | LW | GREENTREE, Kyle | 2007-08 |
| 15, 23, 9 | RW | GREIG, Mark | 1998-01, 2002-03 |
| 32 | D | GRENIER, Martin | 2006-** |
| 25, 34 | RW | GUAY, Paul | 1983-85 |
| 65, 29 | D | GUENIN, Nate | 2006-** |

| NO. | POS. | PLAYER | SEASON (S) |
|---|---|---|---|
| 11, 36 | C | HACHBORN, Len | 1983-85 |
| 33 | G | HACKETT, Jeff | 2003-04 |
| 17, 23, 19 | D | HALE, Larry | 1968-72 |
| 5 | D | HALLER, Kevin | 1994-97 |
| 14 | LW | HAMEL, Denis | 2006-07 |
| 26 | C | HANDZUS, Michal | 2002-06 |
| 6 | D | HANNA, John | 1967-68 |
| 14 | RW | HANNIGAN, Pat | 1967-69 |
| 34 | RW | HARDING, Jeff | 1988-90 |

*Eric Desjardins*

| NO. | POS. | PLAYER | SEASON (S) |
|---|---|---|---|
| 25 | D | HARRIS, Ted | 1974-75 |
| 19 | lw | HARTNELL, Scott | 2007-** |
| 2 | D | HATCHER, Derian | 2005-** |
| 18 | C | HAWERCHUK, Dale | 1995-97 |
| 20 | D | HAWGOOD, Greg | 1992-94 |

# FLYER'D UP!

Trivia, Facts, and Anecdotes for Fans of the Orange and Black.

# FLYERS ALL-TIME ROSTER 1967-2008

| NO. | POS. | PLAYER | SEASON (S) |
|---|---|---|---|
| 38 | RW | HEALY, Paul | 1996-98 |
| 19 | LW | HEISKALA, Earl | 1968-71 |
| 27 | G | HEXTALL, Ron | 1986-92, 94-99 |
| 17 | RW | HICKS, Wayne | 1967-68 |
| 37, 15, 28, 36 | LW | HILL, Al | 1976-82, 86-88 |
| 3 | D | HILLMAN, Larry | 1969-71 |
| 6 | D | HILLMAN, Wayne | 1969-73 |
| 27 | LW | HLAVAC, Jan | 2001-02 |
| 10 | LW | HLUSHKO, Todd | 1993-94 |
| 18 | C | HOEKSTRA, Ed | 1967-68 |
| 24, 34, 35 | D | HOFFMEYER, Bob | 1981-83 |
| 68, 30 | G | HOFFORT, Bruce | 1989-92 |
| 41 | D | HOLAN, Milos | 1993-94 |
| 17 | RW | HOLMGREN, Paul | 1975-84 |
| 24 | D/RW | HOLT, Randy | 1983-84 |
| 43, 21 | LW | HORACEK, Tony | 1989-92 |
| 17 | D | HOSPODAR, Ed | 1984-85, 86-87 |
| 26 | C | HOSTAK, Martin | 1990-92 |
| 35 | G | HOULE, Martin | 2006-** |
| 2 | D | HOWE, Mark | 1982-92 |
| 8 | LW | HOYDA, Dave | 1977-79 |
| 21 | C | HUBACEK, Petr | 2000-01 |
| 47, 44 | D | HUBER, Willie | 1987-88 |
| 5, 2 | D | HUFFMAN, Kerry | 1986-92, 95-96 |
| 5 | D | HUGHES, Brent | 1970-73 |
| 8, 11 | RW | HULL, Jody | 1998-99, 99-01 |
| 26 | D | HYNES, Gord | 1992-93 |

| NO. | POS. | PLAYER | SEASON (S) |
|---|---|---|---|
| 30 | G | INNESS, Gary | 1975-77 |

| NO. | POS. | PLAYER | SEASON (S) |
|---|---|---|---|
| 45, 14 | RW | JENSEN, Chris | 1989-92 |
| 33, 30 | G | JENSEN, Darren | 1984-86 |
| 21, 20 | C | JOHNSON, Jimmy | 1968-72 |
| 5 | D | JOHNSSON, Kim | 2001-06 |
| 47 | LW | JONES, Brad | 1991-92 |
| 20 | RW | JONES, Keith | 1998-01 |
| 51, 29, 6 | D | JONES, Randy | 2003-** |
| 43 | D | JONSSON, Lars | 2006-** |
| 24, 2, 25 | D | JOSEPH, Chris | 1997-99 |
| 20 | C | JOYAL, Eddie | 1971-72 |
| 12 | LW | JUHLIN, Patrik | 1994-96 |

| NO. | POS. | PLAYER | SEASON (S) |
|---|---|---|---|
| 18 | RW | KALLIO, Tomi | 2002-03 |
| 21, 28 | LW | KANE, Boyd | 2003-04, 06-** |

*Sami Kapanen*

| NO. | POS. | PLAYER | SEASON (S) |
|---|---|---|---|
| 24 | LW | KAPANEN, Sami | 2002-08 |
| 15 | C | KASPER, Steve | 1991-93 |
| 36 | RW | KAVANAGH, Pat | 2005-06 |
| 23 | LW/C | KEENAN, Larry | 1971-72 |

| NO. | POS. | PLAYER | SEASON (S) |
|---|---|---|---|
| 9 | LW | KELLY, Bob | 1970-80 |
| 22 | C | KENNEDY, Forbes | 1967-70 |
| 12 | C/RW | KERR, Tim | 1980-91 |
| 26 | C | KINDRACHUK, Orest | 1972-78 |
| 20 | RW | KLATT, Trent | 1995-99 |
| 22 | RW | KNUBLE, Mike | 2005-** |
| 6, 21 | D | KORDIC, Dan | 1991-92, 93-94, 95-99 |
| 25, 15 | LW | KOVALENKO, Andrei | 1998-99 |
| 2 | D | KUCERA, Frantisek | 1996-97 |
| 28 | D | KUKKONEN, Lasse | 2006-** |
| 35 | G | KUNTAR, Les (DNP) | 1994-95 |
| 36, 10, 8, 15 | LW | KUSHNER, Dale | 1990-92 |

*Scott Mellanby*

| NO. | POS. | PLAYER | SEASON (S) |
|---|---|---|---|
| 68, 36, 20 | RW | LACOMBE, Normand | 1990-91 |
| 15, 7 | C | LACROIX, Andre | 1967-71 |
| 32 | LW | LACROIX, Daniel | 1996-98 |
| 33 | G | LaFOREST, Mark | 1987-89 |
| 16 | LW | LAFORGE, Claude | 1967-68 |
| 5 | RW | LAJEUNESSE, Serge | 1973-75 |
| 22 | C | LAMB, Mark | 1993-95 |
| 37 | C | LAMOUREUX, Mitch | 1987-89 |
| 18 | C | LANGKOW, Daymond | 1998-01 |
| 39 | D | LANK, Jeff | 1999-00 |
| 13 | C | LAPOINTE, Claude | 2002-04 |
| 5 | D | LAPOINTE, Rick | 1976-79 |
| 33 | G | LAROCQUE, Michel | 1982-84 |
| 62, 11 | D | LATAL, Jiri | 1989-92 |
| 47 | RW | LAW, Kirby | 2000-01, 2002-04 |
| 18 | LW | LAWLESS, Paul | 1987-88 |
| 5, 27 | RW | LEACH, Reggie | 1974-82 |
| 10 | LW | LeCLAIR, John | 1994-04 |
| 23, 17 | LW | LEFEBVRE, Guillaume | 2001-03 |
| 49 | G | LEIGHTON, Michael | 2006-07 |
| 28 | G | LEMELIN, Rejean (DNP) | 1977-78 |
| 18 | LW | LESUK, Bill | 1970-72 |
| 31 | G | LINDBERGH, Pelle | 1981-86 |
| 88 | C | LINDROS, Eric | 1992-00 |
| 26, 14, 18 | C | LINSEMAN, Ken | 1978-82, 89-90 |
| 35 | G | LITTLE, Neil | 1996-04 |
| 23 | LW | LOMAKIN, Andrei | 1991-93 |
| 18 | LW | LONSBERRY, Ross | 1971-78 |
| 15 | RW | LUCAS, Danny | 1978-79 |
| 15 | rw | LUPUL, Joffrey | 2007-** |

| NO. | POS. | PLAYER | SEASON (S) |
|---|---|---|---|
| 25 | LW | MacADAM, Al | 1973-74 |
| 19, 21 | LW | MacLEISH, Rick | 1970-81, 83-84 |
| 34 | C | MacNEIL, Ian | 2002-03 |
| 19, 4, 21, 24 | D | MacSWEYN, Ralph | 1968-72 |

# FLYER'D UP!

Trivia, Facts, and Anecdotes for Fans of the Orange and Black.

# FLYERS ALL-TIME ROSTER 1967-2008

| NO. | POS. | PLAYER | SEASON (S) |
|---|---|---|---|
| 14 | C | MacTAVISH, Craig | 1994-96 |
| 20 | LW | MAGUIRE, Kevin | 1989-90 |
| 3, 25 | D | MAIR, Jimmy | 1970-72 |
| 43, 23 | D | MALGUNAS, Stewart | 1993-95 |
| 2 | D | MALAKHOV, Vladimir | 2003-04 |
| 28 | C | MANDERVILLE, Kent | 1999-02 |
| 15, 14 | LW | MANELUK, Mike | 1998-99, 99-00 |
| 8, 42 | D | MANTHA, Moe | 1988-89, 91-92 |
| 55 | D | MARKOV, Danny | 2003-04 |
| 8 | D | MARSH, Brad | 1981-88 |
| 24 | D | McALLISTER, Chris | 2000-03 |
| 9 | LW | McAMMOND, Dean | 2000-01 |
| 25, 36, 5 | D | McCARTHY, Kevin | 1977-79, 85-87 |
| 21 | RW | McCARTHY, Sandy | 1998-00 |
| 10 | D | McCRIMMON, Brad | 1982-87 |
| 27, 29 | D | McGILL, Ryan | 1992-95 |
| 3 | D | McGILLIS, Dan | 1997-03 |
| 29 | D | McILHARGEY, Jack | 1974-77, 79-81 |
| 30, 24 | G | McLEOD, Don | 1971-72 |
| 23 | C | MEEHAN, Gerry | 1968-69 |
| 19 | RW | MELLANBY, Scott | 1985-91 |
| 40 | RW | MELOCHE, Eric | 2006-07 |
| 48, 34 | D | MEYER, Freddy | 2003-07 |
| 35, 13 | RW | MICHAYLUK, Dave | 1981-83 |
| 15 | RW | MICKEY, Larry | 1971-72 |
| 4 | D | MISZUK, John | 1968-70 |
| 26 | D | MODRY, Jaroslav | 2007-08 |

*Simon Nolet*

| NO. | POS. | PLAYER | SEASON (S) |
|---|---|---|---|
| 36 | LW | MOKOSAK, Carl | 1985-86 |
| 22 | C | MONTGOMERY, Jim | 1994-96 |
| 39 | G | MOORE, Robbie | 1978-80 |
| 21 | RW | MORRISON, Gary | 1979-82 |
| 8 | RW | MORRISON, Lew | 1969-72 |
| 33 | G | MRAZEK, Jerome | 1975-76 |
| 41 | LW | MULVENNA, Glenn | 1992-93 |
| 67 | G | MUNROE, Scott (DNP) | 2006-** |
| 3 | D | MURPHY, Gord | 1988-92 |
| 39 | C | MURRAY, Marty | 2001-03 |
| 39 | C | MURRAY, Mike | 1987-88 |
| 23, 24 | LW | MURRAY, Pat | 1990-92 |
| 25, 24 | D | MURRAY, Terry | 1975-77, 78-79, 80-81 |
| 18 | RW | MYHRES, Brantt | 1997-98 |
| 31 | G | MYRE, Phil | 1979-81 |
| 42 | LW | NACHBAUR, Don | 1985-90 |
| 5 | D | NATTRESS, Ric | 1992-93 |
| 93 | C | NEDVED, Petr | 2005-07 |
| 44 | D | NIINIMAA, Janne | 1996-98 |
| 30 | G | NIITTYMAKI, Antero | 2003-** |

| NO. | POS. | PLAYER | SEASON (S) |
|---|---|---|---|
| 22, 21, 14, 17 | RW | NOLET, Simon | 1967-74 |
| 77 | C | OATES, Adam | 2001-02 |
| 29 | LW | ODJICK, Gino | 1999-01 |
| 49 | G | OUELLET, Maxime | 2000-01 |
| 17 | LW | OSBURN, Randy | 1974-75 |
| 29 | C | OTTO, Joel | 1995-98 |

*Joel Otto*

| NO. | POS. | PLAYER | SEASON (S) |
|---|---|---|---|
| 21, 12, 32 | RW | PADDOCK, John | 1976-80, 82-83 |
| 20, 18, 19 | RW | PAIEMENT, Rosaire | 1967-70 |
| 30, 1 | G | PARENT, Bernie | 1967-71, 73-79 |
| 77 | D | PARENT, Ryan | 2006-** |
| 7 | LW | PARIZEAU, Michel | 1971-72 |
| 15 | C | PARK, Richard | 1998-99 |
| 12 | C | PASLAWSKI, Greg | 1992-93 |
| 6, 28 | LW | PATERSON, Joe | 1984-85 |
| 34 | D | PATTERSON, Dennis | 1979-80 |
| 41, 14 | LW | PEDERSON, Mark | 1990-93 |
| 33 | G | PEETERS, Pete | 1978-82, 89-91 |
| 49 | G | PELLETIER, Jean-Marc | 1998-00 |
| 19 | D | PELLETIER, Roger | 1967-68 |
| 22 | RW | PELUSO, Mike | 2003-04 |
| 15 | C | PETERS, Garry | 1967-71 |
| 8 | D | PETIT, Michel | 1996-97 |
| 41, 29, 45 | D | PICARD, Alexandre | 2005-08 |
| 42 | LW | PICARD, Michel | 2000-01 |
| 44 | D | PITKANEN, Joni | 2003-07 |
| 38 | C | PLANTE, Derek | 2000-01 |
| 25, 20 | RW | PLANTE, Pierre | 1971-73 |
| 11 | LW | PLETKA, Vaclav | 2001-02 |
| 25 | LW | PODIEN, Shjon | 1994-99 |
| 11 | C | POTULNY, Ryan | 2005-08 |
| 25 | D | POTVIN, Jean | 1971-73 |
| 34, 20 | C | POULIN, Dave | 1982-90 |
| 18 | LW | PRESTON, Yves | 1978-79, 80-81 |
| 25 | C | PRIMEAU, Keith | 1999-06 |
| 28, 54 | D | PRINTZ, David | 2005-07 |
| 14, 26 | LW | PROPP, Brian | 1979-90 |
| 45, 40 | C | PROSPAL, Vaclav | 1996-98, 2007-08 |
| 14, 10, 11 | C | QUINN, Dan | 1991-92, 95-96 |
| 29 | D | RACINE, Yves | 1993-94 |
| 19 | RW | RADIVOJEVIC, Branko | 2003-06 |
| 28 | D | RAGNARSSON, Marcus | 2002-04 |
| 5 | D | RAMAGE, Rob | 1993-94 |
| 19 | LW | RANHEIM, Paul | 2000-03 |
| 3 | D | RATHJE, Mike | 2005-** |

# FLYER'D UP!

Trivia, Facts, and Anecdotes for Fans of the Orange and Black.

# FLYERS ALL-TIME ROSTER 1967-2008

| NO. | POS. | PLAYER | SEASON (S) |
|---|---|---|---|
| 14 | LW | READY, Ryan | 2005-06 |
| 8, 11 | RW | RECCHI, Mark | 1991-95, 98-04 |
| 26 | RW | REID, Darren | 2006-** |
| 19 | RW | RENBERG, Mikael | 1993-97, 98-00 |
| 33 | G | RESCH, Glenn | 1985-87 |
| 18 | C | RICCI, Mike | 1990-92 |
| 18 | C | RICHARDS, Mike | 2005-** |
| 22 | D | RICHARDSON, Luke | 1997-02 |
| 34, 5 | D | RICHTER, Dave | 1985-86 |
| 31 | LW | RITCHIE, Bob | 1976-77 |
| 36 | D | ROBERTS, Gordie | 1987-88 |
| 27 | C | ROBITAILLE, Randy | 2006-07 |
| 9 | RW | ROCHEFORT, Leon | 1967-69 |
| 97 | C | ROENICK, Jeremy | 2001-04 |
| 42 | RW | ROMANIUK, Russ | 1995-96 |
| 48, 34 | D | ROOT, Bill | 1987-88 |
| 10 | LW | ROUPE, Magnus | 1987-88 |
| 33 | G | ROUSSEL, Dominic | 1991-96, 96-97 |
| 36, 3, 5 | D | RUMBLE, Darren | 1990-92, 95-97 |
| 40, 9, 15, 14 | RW | RUZICKA, Stefan | 2005-08 |

*Shjon Podien*

| NO. | POS. | PLAYER | SEASON (S) |
|---|---|---|---|
| 47 | D | SABOL, Shaun | 1989-90 |
| 15 | RW | SACCO, Joe | 2002-03 |
| 25, 11 | RW | SALESKI, Don | 1971-79 |
| 28 | D | SAMUELSSON, Kjell | 1986-92, 95-98 |
| 55 | D | SAMUELSSON, Ulf | 1999-00 |
| 50 | D | SANDELIN, Scott | 1990-91 |
| 8 | LW | SANDERSON, Geoff | 2006-07 |
| 21, 24 | RW | SARRAZIN, Dick | 1968-70, 71-72 |
| 27 | C | SAVAGE, Andre | 2002-03 |
| 49 | LW | SAVAGE, Brian | 2005-06 |
| 10 | RW | SCHMAUTZ, Cliff | 1970-71 |
| 22 | LW | SCHOCK, Danny | 1970-71 |
| 25, 8 | LW | SCHULTZ, Dave | 1971-76 |
| 11 | C | SEABROOKE, Glen | 1986-89 |
| 21 | LW | SECORD, Al | 1988-89 |
| 36, 28 | D | SEIDENBERG, Dennis | 2002-06 |
| 10 | LW | SELBY, Brit | 1967-69 |
| 34, 44 | C | SEMENOV, Anatoli | 1994-96 |
| 30 | G | SETTLEMYRE, Dave (DNP) | 1989-90 |
| 51, 11, 18, 32, 9 | C | SHARP, Patrick | 2002-06 |
| 21 | RW | SIKLENKA, Mike | 2002-03 |
| 11 | C | SILLINGER, Mike | 1997-99 |
| 11 | RW | SIM, Jon | 2005-06 |
| 48 | LW | SIMPSON, Reid | 1991-92 |
| 23 | L/RW | SINISALO, Ilkka | 1981-90 |
| 21 | RW | SIROIS, Bob | 1974-75 |
| 9, 27 | C | SITTLER, Darryl | 1982-84 |

| NO. | POS. | PLAYER | SEASON (S) |
|---|---|---|---|
| 15 | C | SKALDE, Jarrod | 2001-02 |
| 43 | D | SKOLNEY, Wade | 2005-06 |
| 15, 45 | D | SLANEY, John | 2001-02, 2003-04 |
| 24 | LW | SMITH, Derrick | 1984-91 |
| 21 | D | SMITH, Jason | 2007-08 |
| 24, 5 | D | SMITH, Steve | 1981-82, 84-87 |
| 40, 6 | D | SMYTH, Greg | 1986-88 |
| 30 | G | SNOW, Garth | 1995-98 |
| 14 | C | SNUGGERUD, Dave | 1992-93 |
| 30 | G | SODERSTROM, Tommy | 1992-94 |
| 20 | LW | SOMIK, Radovan | 2002-04 |
| 30 | G | ST. CROIX, Rick | 1977-83 |
| 42, 22 | D | ST. JACQUES, Bruno | 2001-03 |
| 23 | RW | STANKIEWICZ, Myron | 1968-69 |
| 6 | D | STANLEY, Allan | 1968-69 |
| 28, 34, 29 | D | STANLEY, Daryl | 1983-84, 85-87 |
| 35 | G | STEPHENSON, Wayne | 1974-79 |
| 41 | D | STEVENS, John | 1986-88 |
| 25 | LW | STEVENS, Kevin | 2000-01 |
| 27 | RW | STEVENSON, Turner | 2005-06 |
| 44 | C | STOCK, P.J. | 2000-01 |
| 35 | G | STORR, Jamie (DNP) | 2005-06 |
| 44 | C | STOTHERS, Mike | 1984-88 |
| 19 | C | STRATTON, Art | 1967-09 |
| 15 | LW | SULLIMAN, Doug | 1988-90 |
| 11, 10 | LW | SUTHERLAND, Bill | 1967-71 |
| 15 | RW | SUTTER, Rich | 1983-86 |
| 14 | C | SUTTER, Ron | 1982-91 |
| 4 | D | SUZOR, Mark | 1976-77 |
| 3, 23 | D | SVOBODA, Petr | 1994-99 |
| 22 | RW | SWARBRICK, George | 1970-71 |
| 23 | D | SYKORA, Michal | 2000-01 |

| NO. | POS. | PLAYER | SEASON (S) |
|---|---|---|---|
| 30 | G | TAYLOR, Bobby | 1971-76 |
| 35, 15 | C | TAYLOR, Mark | 1981-83 |
| 5 | D | TERTYSHNY, Dmitri | 1998-99 |
| 6 | D | THERIEN, Chris | 1994-04, 2005-06 |
| 25 | LW | THORESEN, Patrick | 2007-08 |
| 17 | RW | TIBBETTS, Billy | 2001-02 |
| 2 | D | TILEY, Brad | 2000-01 |

*Keith Primeau*

| NO. | POS. | PLAYER | SEASON (S) |
|---|---|---|---|
| 3 | D | TIMANDER, Mattias | 2003-04 |
| 46 | D | TIMONEN, Jussi | 2006-** |
| 44 | D | TIMONEN, Kimmo | 2007-** |
| 14 | C | TIPPETT, Dave | 1993-94 |
| 22, 92 | RW | TOCCHET, Rick | 1984-92, 99-02 |
| 53 | rw | TOLPEKO, Denis | 2007-08 |
| 37 | C | TOOKEY, Tim | 1986-87 |

# FLYERS ALL-TIME ROSTER 1967-2008

| NO. | POS. | PLAYER | SEASON (S) |
|---|---|---|---|
| 20 | C | UMBERGER, R.J. | 2005-08 |
| 9 | RW | UPSHALL, Scottie | 2006-** |

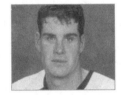

*Chris Therien*

| NO. | POS. | PLAYER | SEASON (S) |
|---|---|---|---|
| 34 | G | VANBIESBROUCK, John | 1998-00 |
| 23, 26 | D | VANDERMEER, Jim | 2002-04, 2007-08 |
| 2 | D | VAN IMPE, Ed | 1967-76 |
| 43, 28, 11 | RW | VERVERGAERT, Dennis | 1978-80 |
| 43 | C | VILGRAIN, Claude | 1993-94 |
| 24, 29 | LW | VOPAT, Roman | 1998-99 |

| NO. | POS. | PLAYER | SEASON (S) |
|---|---|---|---|
| 36 | C | WALZ, Wes | 1991-93 |
| 18 | LW | WARRINER, Todd | 2002-03 |
| 38 | C | WASHBURN, Steve | 1999-00, 2000-01 |
| 20 | D | WATSON, Jimmy | 1972-82 |
| 3, 14 | D | WATSON, Joe | 1967-78 |
| 2 | D | WEINRICH, Eric | 2001-04 |
| 7 | D | WELLS, Jay | 1988-90 |
| 54 | RW | WESENBERG, Brian | 1998-00 |
| 8, 6 | D | WESLEY, Blake | 1979-81 |
| 14, 15 | C | WHITE, Peter | 1998-01, 2003-04 |
| 15, 23 | C | WHITE, Todd | 1999-00 |
| 24 | D | WILKIE, Bob | 1993-94 |
| 35, 34 | C | WILLIAMS, Gordie | 1981-83 |
| 14 | RW | WILLIAMS, Justin | 2000-04 |
| 3 | D | WILSON, Behn | 1978-83 |

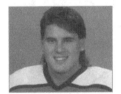

*Peter Zezel*

| NO. | POS. | PLAYER | SEASON (S) |
|---|---|---|---|
| 1 | G | WILSON, Dunc | 1969-70 |
| 32 | RW | WINNES, Chris | 1993-94 |
| 35 | G | WREGGET, Ken | 1988-92 |
| 18 | LW | WRIGHT, Jamie | 2002-03 |
| 20 | LW | WRIGHT, Keith | 1967-68 |
| 10, 15, 21, 20 | C | WRIGHT, Larry | 1971-73, 75-76 |

| NO. | POS. | PLAYER | SEASON (S) |
|---|---|---|---|
| 61 | C | YORK, Mike | 2006-07 |
| 6 | C | YOUNG, Tim | 1984-85 |
| 30 | G | YOUNG, Wendell | 1987-88 |

| NO. | POS. | PLAYER | SEASON (S) |
|---|---|---|---|
| 2, 22 | D | YUSHKEVICH, Dmitry | 1992-95, 02-03 |

| NO. | POS. | PLAYER | SEASON (S) |
|---|---|---|---|
| 24 | D | ZALAPSKI, Zarley | 1999-00 |
| 24 | D | ZEIDEL, Larry | 1967-69 |
| 26 | LW | ZELEPUKIN, Valeri | 1998-00 |
| 40 | LW | ZENT, Jason | 1998-00 |
| 26 | D | ZETTLER, Rob | 1993-95 |
| 25 | C | ZEZEL, Peter | 1984-88 |
| 23 | C | ZHAMNOV, Alexei | 2003-04 |
| 77 | D | ZHITNIK, Alexei | 2006-07 |
| 42, 9 | LW | ZUBRUS, Dainius | 1996-99 |

▨ *Denotes Flyers retired number*
*\*\*:Still active on Flyers roster*
*(DNP): Dressed, but did not play*

171

# FLYER'D UP!

## FLYERS CAPTAINS WORD SEARCH

```
E T U S H T U C H M E H
D T P C I E I A E D S R
I A N I T T O G N A I G
N D S N I D R A J S E D
E N V A N I M P E T S R
E F C M P G N C E I O E
N O L S D R A H C I R T
I R A I S I C I B E D T
L S R S R C H A H S N U
U B K T O T R C P O I S
O E E T I B T T T D L E
P R I M E A U A R E B I
A G S R H E E K C J A B
```

ANGOTTI       VANIMPE       CLARKE
BRIDGMAN      BARBER        POULIN
SUTTER        TOCCHET       DINEEN
LINDROS       DESJARDINS    PRIMEAU
HATCHER       FORSBERG      SMITH
RICHARDS

172

answers on page 182

# FLYERS ALL-TIME REGULAR SEASON RECORDS

## FLYERS ALL-TIME TOP ROOKIE SCORERS 1967-2007

| PLAYER | POS | YEAR | GP | G | A | PTS |
|---|---|---|---|---|---|---|
| Mikael Renberg | RW | 1993-94 | 83 | 38 | 44 | 82 |
| Dave Poulin | C | 1983-84 | 73 | 31 | 45 | 76 |
| Eric Lindros | C | 1992-93 | 61 | 41 | 34 | 75 |
| Brian Propp | LW | 1979-80 | 80 | 34 | 41 | 75 |
| Ron Flockhart | C | 1981-82 | 72 | 33 | 39 | 72 |
| Pelle Eklund | C | 1985-86 | 70 | 15 | 51 | 66 |
| Bill Barber | LW | 1972-73 | 69 | 30 | 34 | 64 |
| Peter Zezel | C | 1984-85 | 65 | 15 | 46 | 61 |
| Andre Lacroix | C | 1968-69 | 75 | 24 | 32 | 56 |
| Serge Bernier | RW | 1970-71 | 77 | 23 | 28 | 51 |
| Ron Sutter | C | 1983-84 | 79 | 19 | 32 | 51 |
| Mel Bridgman | C | 1975-76 | 80 | 23 | 27 | 50 |
| Behn Wilson | D | 1978-79 | 80 | 13 | 36 | 49 |
| Simon Gagne | LW | 1999-2000 | 80 | 20 | 28 | 48 |
| Bobby Clarke | C | 1969-70 | 76 | 15 | 31 | 46 |
| Tim Kerr | C | 1980-81 | 68 | 22 | 23 | 45 |
| Jim Johnson | C | 1968-69 | 69 | 17 | 27 | 44 |
| Thomas Eriksson | D | 1983-84 | 68 | 11 | 33 | 44 |
| Janne Niinimaa | D | 1996-97 | 77 | 4 | 40 | 44 |

## "MOSTS" BY A FLYER IN A SINGLE SEASON:

| GOALS: | | | ASSISTS: | | | POINTS: | | |
|---|---|---|---|---|---|---|---|---|
| Reggie Leach | 61 | 1975-76 | Bobby Clarke | 89 | 1974-75 | Mark Recchi | 123 | 1992-93 |
| Tim Kerr | 58 | 1985-86 | Bobby Clarke | 89 | 1975-76 | Bobby Clarke | 119 | 1975-76 |
| Tim Kerr | 58 | 1986-87 | Mark Recchi | 70 | 1992-93 | Bobby Clarke | 116 | 1974-75 |
| Tim Kerr | 54 | 1983-84 | Bobby Clarke | 68 | 1977-78 | Eric Lindros | 115 | 1995-96 |
| Tim Kerr | 54 | 1984-85 | Ken Linseman | 68 | 1981-82 | Bill Barber | 112 | 1975-76 |
| Mark Recchi | 53 | 1992-93 | Eric Lindros | 68 | 1995-96 | Mark Recchi | 107 | 1993-94 |
| John LeClair | 51 | 1995-96 | Bobby Clarke | 67 | 1972-73 | Bobby Clarke | 104 | 1972-73 |
| John LeClair | 51 | 1997-98 | Mark Recchi | 67 | 1993-94 | Rick MacLeish | 100 | 1972-73 |
| Rick MacLeish | 50 | 1972-73 | Mark Recchi | 63 | 1999-00 | Tim Kerr | 98 | 1984-85 |
| Bill Barber | 50 | 1975-76 | Bobby Clarke | 62 | 1976-77 | Rick MacLeish | 97 | 1976-77 |
| Reggie Leach | 50 | 1979-80 | Bobby Clarke | 62 | 1982-83 | Brian Propp | 97 | 1984-85 |
| John LeClair | 50 | 1996-97 | Rod Brind'Amour | 62 | 1993-94 | Brian Propp | 97 | 1985-86 |
| | | | | | | Rod Brind'Amour | 97 | 1993-94 |
| | | | | | | Eric Lindros | 97 | 1993-94 |
| | | | | | | John LeClair | 97 | 1995-96 |
| | | | | | | John LeClair | 97 | 1996-97 |

## FLYERS ALL-TIME REGULAR SEASON RECORDS 1967-2008

| PLAYER | GOALS | PLAYER | ASSISTS | PLAYER | POINTS |
|---|---|---|---|---|---|
| Bill Barber | 420 | Bobby Clarke | 852 | Bobby Clarke | 1210 |
| Brian Propp | 369 | Brian Propp | 480 | Bill Barber | 883 |
| Tim Kerr | 363 | Bill Barber | 463 | Brian Propp | 849 |
| Bobby Clarke | 358 | Mark Recchi | 395 | Rick MacLeish | 697 |
| John LeClair | 333 | Eric Lindros | 369 | Eric Lindros | 659 |
| Rick MacLeish | 328 | Rick MacLeish | 369 | Tim Kerr | 650 |
| Reggie Leach | 306 | Rod Brind'Amour | 366 | John LeClair | 643 |
| Eric Lindros | 290 | Mark Howe | 342 | Mark Recchi | 627 |
| Rod Brind'Amour | 235 | Pelle Eklund | 334 | Rod Brind'Amour | 601 |
| Mark Recchi | 232 | Gary Dornhoefer | 316 | Gary Dornhoefer | 518 |
| Rick Tocchet | 232 | | | | |

| PLAYER | GAMES | PLAYER | PENALTY MIN. | DEFENSEMEN | G | A | PTS |
|---|---|---|---|---|---|---|---|
| Bobby Clarke | 1144 | Rick Tocchet | 1817 | Mark Howe | 138 | 342 | 480 |
| Bill Barber | 903 | Paul Holmgren | 1600 | Eric Desjardins | 93 | 303 | 396 |
| Brian Propp | 790 | Andre Dupont | 1505 | Tom Bladon | 67 | 163 | 230 |
| Chris Therien | 753 | Bobby Clarke | 1453 | Behn Wilson | 59 | 155 | 214 |
| Joe Watson | 746 | Dave Schultz | 1386 | Joe Watson | 36 | 162 | 198 |
| Bob Kelly | 741 | Dave Brown | 1382 | Bob Dailey | 56 | 138 | 194 |
| Rick MacLeish | 741 | Bob Kelly | 1285 | Doug Crossman | 35 | 158 | 193 |
| Eric Desjardins | 738 | Gary Dornhoefer | 1256 | Brad McCrimmon | 35 | 152 | 187 |
| Gary Dornhoefer | 725 | Craig Berube | 1138 | Jim Watson | 38 | 148 | 186 |
| John LeClair | 649 | Glen Cochrane | 1110 | Andre Dupont | 42 | 135 | 177 |

| LEFT WINGS | G | A | PTS | CENTERS | G | A | PTS | RIGHT WINGS | G | A | PTS |
|---|---|---|---|---|---|---|---|---|---|---|---|
| Bill Barber | 420 | 463 | 883 | Bobby Clarke | 358 | 852 | 1210 | Tim Kerr | 363 | 287 | 650 |
| Brian Propp | 369 | 480 | 849 | Rick MacLeish | 328 | 369 | 697 | Mark Recchi | 232 | 395 | 627 |
| John LeClair | 333 | 310 | 643 | Eric Lindros | 290 | 369 | 659 | Gary Dornhoefer | 202 | 316 | 518 |
| Murray Craven | 152 | 272 | 424 | Rod Brind'Amour | 235 | 366 | 601 | Reggie Leach | 306 | 208 | 514 |
| *Simon Gagne | 208 | 202 | 410 | Pelle Eklund | 118 | 334 | 452 | Rick Tocchet | 232 | 276 | 508 |
| Ross Lonsberry | 144 | 170 | 314 | Dave Poulin | 161 | 233 | 394 | Ilkka Sinisalo | 199 | 209 | 408 |
| Bob Kelly | 128 | 168 | 296 | Ron Sutter | 137 | 223 | 360 | Paul Holmgren | 138 | 171 | 309 |
| Derrick Smith | 80 | 87 | 167 | Mel Bridgman | 119 | 205 | 324 | Mikael Renberg | 128 | 168 | 296 |
| Jean-Guy Gendron | 69 | 86 | 155 | Peter Zezel | 91 | 170 | 261 | Don Saleski | 118 | 117 | 235 |
| Lindsay Carson | 61 | 76 | 137 | Orest Kindrachuk | 79 | 181 | 260 | Simon Nolet | 93 | 108 | 201 |

| POWER PLAY | GOALS | SHORTHANDED | GOALS | HAT TRICKS | |
|---|---|---|---|---|---|
| Tim Kerr | 145 | Bobby Clarke | 32 | Tim Kerr | 17 |
| Bill Barber | 104 | Bill Barber | 31 | Rick MacLeish | 12 |
| Brian Propp | 103 | Dave Poulin | 27 | John LeClair | 11 |
| John LeClair | 102 | Mark Howe | 24 | Eric Lindros | 11 |
| Bobby Clarke | 99 | Rick MacLeish | 21 | Brian Propp | 8 |
| Rick MacLeish | 98 | Brian Propp | 20 | Rick Tocchet | 8 |
| Eric Lindros | 82 | Rod Brind'Amour | 18 | Reggie Leach | 7 |
| Reggie Leach | 79 | *Mike Richards | 12 | Bill Barber | 6 |
| Rod Brind'Amour | 75 | Don Saleski | 11 | Bobby Clarke | 5 |
| Mark Recchi | 74 | Ilkka Sinisalo | 11 | Kevin Dineen | 5 |
| Rick Tocchet | 64 | Mark Recchi | 10 | Dave Poulin | 5 |
| *Simon Gagne | 55 | Murray Craven | 9 | | |
| Ilkka Sinisalo | 45 | | | | |
| Gary Dornhoefer | 44 | | | | |
| Pelle Eklund | 41 | | | | |

### GOALTENDERS

| GAMES | | SHUTOUTS | | AVERAGE (50 OR MORE GAMES) | | WINS | |
|---|---|---|---|---|---|---|---|
| Ron Hextall | 489 | Bernie Parent | 50 | Roman Cechmanek | 1.96 | Ron Hextall | 240 |
| Bernie Parent | 486 | Roman Cechmanek | 20 | John Vanbiesbrouck | 2.19 | Bernie Parent | 232 |
| Doug Favell | 215 | Ron Hextall | 18 | Bernie Parent | 2.42 | Wayne Stephenson | 93 |
| Pete Peeters | 179 | Doug Favell | 16 | Brian Boucher | 2.45 | Roman Cechmanek | 92 |
| Wayne Stephenson | 165 | Bob Froese | 12 | Garth Snow | 2.59 | Bob Froese | 92 |
| Roman Cechmanek | 163 | Wayne Stephenson | 10 | Robert Esche | 2.65 | Pelle Lindbergh | 87 |
| Pelle Lindbergh | 157 | John Vanbiesbrouck | 9 | *Martin Biron | 2.68 | Pete Peeters | 85 |

* Still active on Flyers roster

# FLYER'D UP!

Trivia, Facts, and Anecdotes for Fans of the Orange and Black.

# FLYERS ALL-TIME REGULAR SEASON STREAKS 1967-2008

## TEAM RECORDS: STREAKS

### LONGEST...

### WIN STREAKS

| | |
|---|---|
| 13 Games | Oct. 19, 1985 through Nov. 17, 1985 |
| 11 Games | March 5, 1985 through March 24, 1985 |
| 10 Games | Dec. 22, 1982 through Jan. 13, 1983 |
| 9 Games | Oct. 25, 1979 through Nov. 15, 1979 |
| 9 Games | April 2, 1995 through April 22, 1995 |

### WIN STREAKS AT HOME

| | |
|---|---|
| 20 Games | Jan. 4, 1976 through April 3, 1976 |
| 14 Games | Feb. 10, 1985 through April 4, 1985 |
| 11 Games | Feb. 13, 1975 through March 30, 1975 |
| 11 Games | Nov. 28, 1976 through Jan. 16, 1977 |
| 11 Games | Oct. 19, 1985 through Nov. 27, 1985 |

### WIN STREAKS ON THE ROAD

| | |
|---|---|
| 8 Games | Dec. 22, 1982 through Jan. 16, 1983 |
| 7 Games | Oct. 12, 1985 through Nov. 16, 1985 |
| 6 Games | Jan. 22, 1980 through Feb. 9, 1980 |
| 6 Games | March 5, 1985 through March 23, 1985 |
| 6 Games | Jan. 2, 2003 through Jan. 21, 2003 |
| 6 Games | Dec. 13, 2005 through Dec. 29, 2005 |
| 6 Games | Jan. 5, 2008 through Feb. 5, 2008 |

### LOSING STREAKS

| | |
|---|---|
| 9 Games | Dec. 8, 2006 through Dec. 27, 2006 |
| 7 Games | Jan. 4, 2007 through Jan. 18, 2007 |
| 6 Games | March 25, 1970 through April 4, 1970 |
| 6 Games | Dec. 5, 1992 through Dec. 17, 1992 |
| 6 Games | Jan. 25, 1994 through Feb. 5, 1994 |

### LOSING STREAKS AT HOME

| | |
|---|---|
| 8 Games | Dec. 9, 2006 through Jan. 27, 2007 |
| 5 Games | Jan. 30, 1969 through Feb. 15, 1969 |
| 5 Games | Dec. 19, 1989 through Jan. 23, 1990 |
| 5 Games | Feb. 6, 2008 through Feb. 21, 2008 |
| 4 Games | 4 times |

### LOSING STREAKS ON THE ROAD

| | |
|---|---|
| 8 Games | Oct. 25, 1972 through Nov. 26, 1972 |
| 8 Games | March 3, 1988 through March 29, 1988 |
| 7 Games | Dec. 28, 1991 through Jan. 25, 1992 |
| 6 Games | 8 times |

### TIE STREAKS

| | |
|---|---|
| 4 Games | Jan. 2, 1969 through Jan. 8, 1969 |
| 4 Games | Dec. 8, 1991 through Dec. 15, 1991 |
| 3 Games | Feb. 27, 1969 through March 2, 1969 |
| 3 Games | Oct. 23, 1969 through Oct. 30, 1969 |
| 3 Games | March 1, 1970 through March 7, 1970 |
| 3 Games | Jan. 20, 1971 through Jan. 23, 1971 |
| 3 Games | Jan. 18, 1979 through Jan. 21, 1979 |
| 3 Games | Dec. 1, 1979 through Dec. 4, 1979 |
| 3 Games | Dec. 17, 1983 through Dec. 21, 1983 |
| 3 Games | Jan. 4, 1996 through Jan. 11, 1996 |
| 3 Games | March 6, 1999 through March 9, 1999 |
| 3 Games | Nov. 13, 2002 through Nov. 16, 2002 |

### TIE STREAKS AT HOME

| | |
|---|---|
| 4 Games | Oct. 19, 1969 through Oct. 30, 1969 |
| 3 Games | Jan. 11, 1979 through Jan. 18, 1979 |
| 3 Games | Dec. 8, 1991 through Dec. 14, 1991 |
| 3 Games | Nov. 13, 2002 through Nov. 21, 2002 |

### TIE STREAKS ON THE ROAD

| | |
|---|---|
| 4 Games | March 1, 1969 through March 15, 1969 |
| 3 Games | Dec. 27, 1968 through Jan. 8, 1969 |
| 3 Games | Feb. 21, 1976 through Feb. 28, 1976 |
| 3 Games | Nov. 24, 1979 through Dec. 16, 1979 |
| 3 Games | Dec. 12, 2000 through Dec. 19, 2000 |

### UNDEFEATED STREAKS

| | |
|---|---|
| 35 Games | Oct. 14, 1979 through Jan. 6, 1980 (25-0-10) |
| 23 Games | Jan. 29, 1976 through March 18, 1976 (17-0-6) |
| 20 Games | Nov. 16, 1976 through Jan. 1, 1977 (15-0-5) |
| 17 Games | Nov. 30, 1996 through Jan. 7, 1997 (14-0-3) |
| 15 Games | Dec. 12, 1998 through Jan. 13, 1999 (10-0-5) |

### UNDEFEATED STREAKS AT HOME

| | |
|---|---|
| 26 Games | Oct. 11, 1979 through Feb. 3, 1980 (19-0-7) |
| 21 Games | Oct. 17, 1976 through Jan. 16, 1977 (20-0-1) |
| 20 Games | Jan. 4, 1976 through April 3, 1976 (20-0-0) |
| 16 Games | Oct. 19, 1980 through Dec. 18, 1980 (14-0-2) |
| 15 Games | Feb. 7, 1985 through April 4, 1985 (14-0-1) |
| 15 Games | Oct. 28, 1999 through Jan. 8, 2000 (12-0-3) |

### UNDEFEATED STREAKS ON THE ROAD

| | |
|---|---|
| 16 Games | Oct. 20, 1979 through Jan. 6, 1980 (11-0-5) |
| 12 Games | Nov. 30, 1996 through Jan. 29, 1997 (8-0-4) |
| 11 Games | Jan. 29, 1976 through March 16, 1976 (5-0-6) |
| 10 Games | Nov. 26, 1976 through Jan. 1, 1977 (6-0-4) |
| 10 Games | Feb. 26, 1977 through April 3, 1977 (6-0-4) |
| 10 Games | Dec. 8, 1998 through Jan. 18, 1999 (7-0-3) |

### WINLESS STREAKS

| | |
|---|---|
| 12 Games | Feb. 24, 1999 through March 16, 1999 (0-8-4) |
| 11 Games | Nov. 21, 1968 through Dec. 14, 1968 (0-9-2) |
| 11 Games | Dec. 10, 1970 through Jan. 3, 1971 (0-9-2) |
| 10 Games | Dec. 31, 1989 through Jan. 23, 1990 (0-7-3) |
| 10 Games | Dec. 2, 2006 through Dec. 27, 2006 (0-9-1) |
| 10 Games | Feb. 6, 2008 through Feb. 23, 2008 |

### WINLESS STREAKS AT HOME

| | |
|---|---|
| 13 Games | Nov. 29, 2006 through Feb. 8, 2007 (0-9-4) |
| 8 Games | Dec. 19, 1968 through Jan. 18, 1969 (0-4-4) |
| 8 Games | Nov. 17, 1991 through Dec. 14, 1991 (0-4-4) |
| 7 Games | Dec. 2, 1990 through Jan. 13, 1991 (0-4-3) |
| 6 Games | Nov. 21, 1968 through Dec. 12, 1968 (0-5-1) |
| 6 Games | Nov. 7, 2002 through Dec. 2, 2002 (0-2-3-1) |
| 6 Games | Nov. 2, 2006 through Nov. 22, 2006 (0-4-2) |
| 6 Games | Feb. 6, 2008 through Feb. 23, 2008 |

### WINLESS STREAKS ON THE ROAD

| | |
|---|---|
| 19 Games | Oct. 23, 1971 through Jan. 27, 1972 (0-15-4) |
| 15 Games | Jan. 15, 1969 through March 16, 1969 (0-7-8) |
| 11 Games | Oct. 20, 1972 through Dec. 13, 1972 (0-9-2) |
| 10 Games | Jan. 19, 1982 through Feb. 24, 1982 (0-7-3) |
| 10 Games | Dec. 27, 1991 through Feb. 4, 1992 (0-8-2) |

# FLYER'D UP!

Trivia, Facts, and Anecdotes for Fans of the Orange and Black.

# FLYERS ALL-TIME PLAYOFF LEADERS 1967-2008

## POINTS BY POSITION

### CENTER

| | GP | G | A | PTS |
|---|---|---|---|---|
| Bobby Clarke | 136 | 42 | 77 | 119 |
| Rick MacLeish | 108 | 53 | 52 | 105 |
| Eric Lindros | 50 | 24 | 33 | 57 |
| Ken Linseman | 41 | 11 | 42 | 53 |
| Rod Brind'Amour | 57 | 24 | 27 | 51 |

### RIGHT WING

| | GP | G | A | PTS |
|---|---|---|---|---|
| Tim Kerr | 73 | 39 | 31 | 70 |
| Reggie Leach | 91 | 47 | 22 | 69 |
| Rick Tocchet | 95 | 27 | 33 | 60 |
| Paul Holmgren | 67 | 19 | 3150 | |
| Mark Recchi | 65 | 19 | 20 | 39 |

### LEFT WING

| | GP | G | A | PTS |
|---|---|---|---|---|
| Brian Propp | 116 | 52 | 60 | 112 |
| Bill Barber | 129 | 53 | 55 | 108 |
| John LeClair | 116 | 35 | 39 | 74 |
| Ross Lonsberry | 83 | 19 | 22 | 41 |
| *Simon Gagne | 65 | 20 | 11 | 31 |

### DEFENSE

| | GP | G | A | PTS |
|---|---|---|---|---|
| Mark Howe | 82 | 8 | 45 | 53 |
| Eric Desjardins | 97 | 14 | 37 | 51 |
| Bob Dailey | 56 | 10 | 30 | 40 |
| Jim Watson | 101 | 5 | 34 | 39 |
| Behn Wilson | 43 | 8 | 24 | 32 |
| Tom Bladon | 78 | 8 | 24 | 32 |

## CATEGORY LEADERS

### GOAL LEADERS

| | |
|---|---|
| Bill Barber | 53 |
| Rick MacLeish | 53 |
| Brian Propp | 52 |
| Reggie Leach | 47 |
| Bobby Clarke | 42 |

### ASSIST LEADERS

| | |
|---|---|
| Bobby Clarke | 77 |
| Brian Propp | 60 |
| Bill Barber | 55 |
| Rick MacLeish | 52 |
| Mark Howe | 45 |

### GAMES PLAYED

| | |
|---|---|
| Bobby Clarke | 136 |
| Bill Barber | 129 |
| John LeClair | 116 |
| Brian Propp | 116 |
| Rick MacLeish | 108 |
| Andre Dupont | 108 |

### GOALTENDER WINS

| | |
|---|---|
| Ron Hextall | 45 |
| Bernie Parent | 35 |
| Robert Esche | 13 |
| Pelle Lindbergh | 12 |
| Brian Boucher | 11 |
| Pete Peeters | 11 |

## FLYERS ALL-TIME PLAYOFF GAME-WINNING GOALS 1967-2007

| | | | | | |
|---|---|---|---|---|---|
| Rick MacLeish | 10# | Paul Holmgren | 2 | Kim Johnsson | 1 |
| Reggie Leach | 8 | Bob Kelly | 2# | Sami Kapanen | 1 |
| John LeClair | 8 | Trent Klatt | 2 | *Mike Knuble | 1 |
| Bobby Clarke | 7 | Daymond Langkow | 2 | *Joffrey Lupul | 1 |
| Brian Propp | 7 | Brad McCrimmon | 2 | Danny Markov | 1 |
| Bill Barber | 6 | Shjon Podein | 2 | Scott Mellanby | 1 |
| Tim Kerr | 6 | Jeremy Roenick | 2 | Gord Murphy | 1 |
| Rick Tocchet | 6 | Derrick Smith | 2 | Don Nachbaur | 1 |
| Ken Linseman | 5 | R.J. Umberger | 2 | Janne Niinimaa | 1 |
| Ross Lonsberry | 5 | Behn Wilson | 2 | Joel Otto | 1 |
| Ilkka Sinisalo | 5 | Peter Zezel | 2 | Rosaire Paiement | 1 |
| Eric Desjardins | 4 | Shawn Antoski | 1 | Marcus Ragnarsson | 1 |
| Gary Dornhoefer | 4 | Todd Bergen | 1 | Leon Rochefort | 1 |
| Eric Lindros | 4 | Craig Berube | 1 | Kjell Samuelsson | 1 |
| Keith Primeau | 4 | Don Blackburn | 1 | Dave Schultz | 1 |
| Mel Bridgman | 3 | Tom Bladon | 1 | Ron Sutter | 1 |
| *Danny Briere | 3 | *Jeff Carter | 1 | Chris Therien | 1 |
| *Simon Gagne | 3 | Terry Crisp | 1 | Mattias Timander | 1 |
| Orest Kindrachuk | 3 | J.J. Daigneault | 1 | *Scottie Upshall | 1 |
| Dave Poulin | 3 | Rob DiMaio | 1 | Jim Watson | 1 |
| Mark Recchi | 3 | Kevin Dineen | 1 | Justin Williams | 1 |
| Don Saleski | 3 | Pelle Eklund | 1 | Dmitry Yushkevich | 1 |
| Rod Brind'Amour | 2 | Ruslan Fedotenko | 1 | Alexei Zhamnov | 1 |
| Murray Craven | 2 | Bill Flett | 1 | Valeri Zelepukin | 1 |
| Bob Dailey | 2 | Kevin Haller | 1 | Dainius Zubrus | 1 |
| Andy Delmore | 2 | Michal Handzus | 1 | | |
| Andre Dupont | 2 | Dale Hawerchuk | 1 | # Includes Stanley Cup Winner |
| Karl Dykhuis | 2 | Al Hill | 1 | * Still active on Flyers roster |
| Peter Forsberg | 2 | Mark Howe | 1 | | |

# FLYERS PENALTY SHOTS 1967-2008

| PLAYER | DATE | OPPONENT | HOME/AWAY | GOALTENDER | RESULT |
|--------|------|----------|-----------|------------|--------|
| Bill Clement | Mar. 7, 1974 | Detroit | Home | Jim Rutherford | No Goal |
| Orest Kindrachuk | Nov. 9, 1974 | Washington | Home | Michel Belhumeur | Goal |
| Bill Barber* | May 7, 1975 | NY Islanders | Away | Glenn Resch | No Goal |
| Orest Kindrachuk | Oct. 15, 1977 | Pittsburgh | Home | Dunc Wilson | No Goal |
| Rick MacLeish | Mar. 20, 1978 | NY Islanders | Home | Billy Smith | Goal |
| Ilkka Sinisalo | Oct. 11, 1981 | Pittsburgh | Home | Paul Harrison | Goal |
| Behn Wilson | Dec. 17, 1981 | Buffalo | Home | Don Edwards | Goal |
| Brian Propp | Jan. 4, 1983 | Vancouver | Home | Ken Ellacott | Goal |
| Ron Sutter | Nov. 18, 1984 | NY Islanders | Home | Kelly Hrudey | No Goal |
| Ron Sutter* | May 28, 1985 | Edmonton | Away | Grant Fuhr | No Goal |
| Dave Poulin* | May 30, 1985 | Edmonton | Away | Grant Fuhr | No Goal |
| Brian Propp | Dec. 19, 1985 | New Jersey | Home | Glenn Resch | No Goal |
| Dave Poulin | Mar. 6, 1986 | Toronto | Home | Don Edwards | No Goal |
| Rick Tocchet | Jan. 6, 1987 | New Jersey | Home | Craig Billington | No Goal |
| Pelle Eklund | Jan. 14, 1990 | NY Rangers | Away | Mike Richter | No Goal |
| Keith Acton | Mar. 25, 1990 | NY Rangers | Away | John Vanbiesbrouck | Goal |
| Mike Ricci | Nov. 17, 1990 | New Jersey | Away | Chris Terreri | No Goal |
| Murray Craven | Dec. 23, 1990 | Montreal | Home | Andre Racicot | Goal |
| Norman Lacombe | Feb. 5, 1991 | Los Angeles | Home | Kelly Hrudey | Goal |
| Murray Craven | Oct. 13, 1991 | New Jersey | Home | Chris Terreri | No Goal |
| Eric Lindros | Dec. 26, 1992 | Washington | Away | Don Beaupre | Goal |
| Mark Recchi | Feb. 6, 1995 | Ottawa | Away | Don Beaupre | No Goal |
| Eric Lindros* | May 11, 1997 | Buffalo | Away | Steve Shields | Goal |
| Trent Klatt | Oct. 1, 1997 | Florida | Home | John Vanbiesbrouck | No Goal |
| Valeri Zelepukin | Oct. 30, 1999 | New Jersey | Home | Martin Brodeur | No Goal |
| Eric Desjardins * | Apr. 16, 2000 | Buffalo | Away | Dominik Hasek | No Goal |
| Mark Recchi* | Apr. 11, 2001 | Buffalo | Home | Dominik Hasek | No Goal |
| Michal Handzus | Dec. 5, 2002 | NY Rangers | Home | Dan Blackburn | Goal |
| Simon Gagne | Feb. 21, 2004 | Atlanta | Home | Pasi Nurminen | Goal |
| Alexei Zhamnov | Feb. 24, 2004 | Chicago | Home | Michael Leighton | No Goal |
| Peter Forsberg | Oct. 27, 2005 | Florida | Home | Roberto Luongo | No Goal |
| R.J. Umberger | Nov. 18, 2005 | Atlanta | Home | Michael Garnett | No Goal |
| Mike Richards | Oct. 17, 2006 | Buffalo | Away | Ryan Miller | No Goal |
| R.J. Umberger | Dec. 21, 2006 | Montreal | Away | David Aebischer | No Goal |
| Dmitry Afanasenkov | Feb. 17, 2007 | NY Rangers | Away | Stephen Valiquette | No Goal |
| Mike Richards | Nov. 21, 2007 | Carolina | Away | Cam Ward | No Goal |
| Danny Briere | Dec. 16, 2007 | New Jersey | Away | Martin Brodeur | No Goal |
| Joffrey Lupul | Dec. 29, 2007 | Tampa Bay | Away | Karri Ramo | Goal |
| Mike Richards * | Apr. 15, 2008 | Washington | Home | Cristobal Huet | Goal |

*Playoffs*

NOTES: The Flyers have connected on 14 of 39 penalty shot attempts, 35.9%. Michal Handzus' attempt on December 5, 2002, was the Flyers' first penalty shot attempt in regular season overtime. It was the seventh penalty shot attempt in regular season overtime since the NHL instituted regular season overtime for the 1983-84 season. It was only the second successful penalty shot attempt in regular season overtime in NHL history – Nashville's David Legwand scored on the Rangers' Kirk McLean to give the Predators a 3-2 win at New York on December 23, 2000. Eric Desjardins and Behn Wilson are the only Flyers defensemen ever to attempt a penalty shot. Ilkka Sinisalo became only the third player in NHL history to score his first goal on a penalty shot. The others were Ralph Bowman of the St. Louis Eagles, when in 1934-35 he recorded the first-ever successful penalty shot in the NHL, and Phil Hoene of the Los Angeles Kings in 1973-74. With his goal vs. Washington on April 15, 2008, Mike Richards' became only the second player in NHL history to record their first career NHL playoff goal on a penalty shot (Minnesota's Wayne Connolly in 1968).

# FLYER'D UP!

Trivia, Facts, and Anecdotes for Fans of the Orange and Black.

# FLYERS FIFTY GOAL SCORERS

*from left to right: Bill Barber, Tim Kerr, Reggie Leach, John LeClair, Rick MacLeish, Mark Recchi*

# FLYER'D UP!

Trivia, Facts, and Anecdotes for Fans of the Orange and Black.

# TRIVIA ANSWER KEY

**(P. 26-28 ) 60's and 70's Trivia  TRIVIA**

| 1.B | 2.C | 3.D | 4.A | 5.D | 6.D | 7.B | 8.C | 9.A | 10.D |
|-----|-----|-----|-----|-----|-----|-----|-----|-----|------|
| 11.A | 12.C | 13.B | 14.B | 15.C | 16.C | 17.A | 18.D | 19.D | 20. D |
| 21.B | 22.A | 23.C | 24.C | 25.B | | | | | |

**(P. 34-36) 80's TRIVIA**

| 1.D | 2.A | 3.B | 4.B | 5.D | 6.C | 7.C | 8.A | 9.C | 10.B |
|-----|-----|-----|-----|-----|-----|-----|-----|-----|------|
| 11.D | 12.A | 13.C | 14.D | 15.C | 16.A | 17.B | 18.C | 19.D | 20. A |
| 21.D | 22.A | 23.D | 24.C | 25.C | 26.C | 27.B | | | |

**(P. 44-46) 90's TRIVIA**

| 1.D | 2.A | 3.C | 4.D | 5.B | 6.C | 7.B | 8.A | 9.D | 10.C |
|-----|-----|-----|-----|-----|-----|-----|-----|-----|------|
| 11.A | 12.B | 13.B | 14.D | 15.C | 16.A | 17.C | 18.B | 19.A | 20. D |
| 21.C | 22.D | 23.C | 24.B | 25.A | 26.B | | | | |

**(P. 56-58) 2000's TRIVIA**

| 1.A | 2.B | 3.C | 4.B | 5.D | 6.D | 7.D | 8.C | 9.A | 10.B |
|-----|-----|-----|-----|-----|-----|-----|-----|-----|------|
| 11.C | 12.A | 13.D | 14.A | 15.C | 16.B | 17.C | 18.A | 19.B | 20. D |
| 21.C | 22.C | 23.C | 24.A | | | | | | |

**(P. 86-88)  BEFORE OR AFTER THEY WERE FLYERS**

| 1.A | 2.D | 3.C | 4.C | 5.B | 6.D | 7.A | 8.A | 9.A | 10.C |
|-----|-----|-----|-----|-----|-----|-----|-----|-----|------|
| 11.B | 12.B | 13.D | 14.D | 15.A | 16.C | 17.B | 18.C | 19.C | 20.A |

**(P. 92-94) FLYERS FIRSTS**

| 1.C | 2.A | 3.C | 4.D | 5.D | 6.A | 7.A | 8.A | 9.C | 10.D |
|-----|-----|-----|-----|-----|-----|-----|-----|-----|------|
| 11.B | 12.A | 13.C | 14.A | 15.B | 16.A | 17.D | 18.C | 19.B | 20. C |
| 21.B | 22.C | 23.A | 24.C | 25.B | 26.B | | | | |

**(P. 98-100) HAT TRICKS TRIVIA**

| 1.A | 2.D | 3.C | 4.B | 5.B | 6.C | 7.D | 8.A | 9.D | 10.C |
|-----|-----|-----|-----|-----|-----|-----|-----|-----|------|
| 11.D | 12.D | 13.C | 14.B | 15.B | 16.D | 17.A | 18.A | 19.C | 21.A |
| 22.B | 23.A | 24.C | 25.A | | | | | | |

# FLYER'D UP!

Trivia, Facts, and Anecdotes for Fans of the Orange and Black.

## FLYERS PLAYERS NAME SCRAMBLE   *(Answers from pgs 106-107)*

1.DMITRY AFANASENKOV
2.JEFF CHYCHRUN
3.NOLAN BAUMGARTNER
4.BARRY DEAN
5.ERIC DESJARDINS
6.THOMAS ERIKSSON
7.RUSLAN FEDOTENKO
8.MARTIN GRENIER
9.LEN HACHBORN
10.GARY INNES
11.PATRIK JUHLIN
12.ANDREI KOVALENKO
13.CLAUDE LAFORGE
14.GLENN MULVENNA
15.RIC NATTRESS
16.GINO ODJICK
17.TOM BLADON
18.SIMON NOLET
19.RYAN POTULNY
20. DAN QUINN
21.DAVE SNUGGERUD
22.TIM TOOKEY
23.SCOTTIE UPSHALL
24.ROMAN VOPAT
25.WES WALZ
26.CHRIS WINNES
27.DMITRY YUSHKEVICH
28.JASON ZENT
29.ZARLEY ZALAPSKI
30. JOHN VANBIESBROUCK

### *(P. 122-123) THE NUMBER GAME*

| 1.A | 2.D | 3.B | 4.B | 5.D | 6.B | 7.A | 8.C | 9.B&C | 10.C |
|-----|-----|-----|-----|-----|-----|-----|-----|-------|------|
| 11.D | 12.B | 13.C | 14.C | 15.C | 16.D | 17.A | 18.D | 19.B | 20. C |

### *(P. 126-128) THE STREAK*

| 1.A | 2.A | 3.C | 4.B | 5.D | 6.C | 7.A | 8.D | 9.A |
|-----|-----|-----|-----|-----|-----|-----|-----|-----|
| 10.A & C | | 11.B | 12.D | 13.C | 14.C | 15.D | 16.D | |

### *(P. 134-136) TRADES TRIVIA*

| 1.C | 2.A | 3.A | 4.C | 5.C | 6.D | 7.D | 8.C | 9.B | 10.A |
|-----|-----|-----|-----|-----|-----|-----|-----|-----|------|
| 11.B | 12.A | 13.A | 14.B | 15.A | 16.D | 17.C | 18.C | 19.B | 20. D |
| 21.A | 22.A | 23.C | 24.B | 25.D | | | | | |

### *(P. 142-144) BOBBY CLARKE TRIVIA*

| 1.A | 2.A | 3.A&B | 4.D | 5.D | 6.B | 7.B | 8.B | 9.C | 10.C |
|-----|-----|-------|-----|-----|-----|-----|-----|-----|------|
| 11.A | 12.A | 13.D | 14.C | 15.D | 16.B | 17.B | 18.A | 19.A | 20. D |
| 21.B | 22.C | 23.C | | | | | | | |

# FLYER'D UP!

Trivia, Facts, and Anecdotes for Fans of the Orange and Black.

## (P. 150-152) TROPHIES AND AWARDS TRIVIA

| 1.A | 2.C | 3.B | 4.A | 5.B | 6.D | 7.A | 8.A | 9.D | 10.B |
| 11.A | 12.D | 13.D | 14.B | 15.D | 16.A | 17.C | 18.B | 19.A | 20. B |
| 21.C | 22. A | 23. D | 24. A | 25. D | 26. C | | | | |

## NICKNAMES (Answers from pg. 114)

| | | |
|---|---|---|
| A. | Bob Kelly | The Hound |
| B. | Dave Schultz | The Hammer |
| C. | Larry Goodenough | Izzy |
| D. | Mark LaForest | Trees |
| E. | Ed Hospodar | Boxcar |
| F. | Reggie Leach | The Rifle |
| G. | Eric Lindros | The Big E |
| H. | Ken Linesman | The Rat |
| I. | Chris Therien | Bundy |
| J. | Bobby Taylor | Chief |
| K. | John Vanbiesbrouck | Beezer |
| L. | Andre Dupont | Moose |
| M. | Don Saleski | Big Bird |
| N. | Bob Dailey | The Count |
| O. | Joe Watson | Thundermouth |
| P. | Glen Resch | Chico |
| Q. | Eric Desjardins | Rico |
| R. | Brian Boucher | Boosh |
| S. | Bob Froese | Frosty |
| T. | Miroslav Dvorak | Cookie |
| U. | Jeremy Roenick | JR |
| V. | Brad McCrimmon | The Beast |
| W. | Bill Flett | Cowboy |
| X. | Simon Gagne | Gags |
| Y. | Dominic Roussel | Roo |
| Z. | Kjell Samuelsson | Sammy |

# FLYER'D UP!

## *Word Search Answer Keys*

### FLYERS GOALTENDERS WORD SEARCH
#### page 47

```
U E S T M T R K A M P R K C N
I M N O O E S C H E N O R I B
B K O B E L H U M E U R E N S
I R A R T G B O U C H E R N I
E S E M T S E R O F A L O E H
P C T H Y S T B G I C W N S C
N E H E G T R S S W K S I S S
U T E E P R T E G G E R W E E
W U X T C H E I D N T O T F R
O T T I E H E B I O T U E F P
S E A F O R M N D N S S K A R
A A L Y Y R S A S N E S R V I
H T L M L K C V N O I E U E N
E H O F F O R T R E N L B L H
G A M B L E R F S T K R T L W
```

### NHL TEAMS WORD SEARCH
#### page 95

```
C L R G R F M T G O F H Y X A T
D H Y N E T I O I S G S C I W L
N Y I S L A N D E R S R O N A F
A C P C W R N E U U N E L E T T
S C O E A A E B W A I G U O T N
H A N L T G S V O J A N M H O E
V L T O O T O H U N E A B P A T
I G N L T R T T I O O R U A M E
L A I I A N A L N N C Y S O A S
L R P U M N O D C O G N N E T O
E Y A A P R T M O A R T A I Y J N
B U F F A L O A D J R O O V O N
M R H C B S U O A P R R T N T A
M I E H A N A Y A S T L O U I S
O O F N Y O R L O E B O S T O N
L E L F L O R I D A S A L L A D
```

### FLYERS HEAD COACHES WORD SEARCH
#### page 141

```
Q O B N I O L O N N N
U N A B S N E V E T S
I I R S A O O R L I H
N N B N I M G S L O E
N E E A O M T Q A C R
O E R E L A P N A S O
K N S O S C U S S A A
T I H I T C H C O C K
S D U R A M S E Y N I
E K H Y A R R U M S B
N R M N E I L S O N S
```

### FLYERS CAPTAINS WORD SEARCH
#### page 172

```
E T U S H T U C H M E H
D T P C I E I A E D S R
I A N I T T O G N A I G
N D S N I D R A J S E D
E N V A N I M P E T S R
E F C M P G N C E I O E
N O L S D R A H C I R T
I R A I S I C I B E D T
L S R S R C H A H S N U
U B K T O T R C P O I S
O E E T I B T T T D L E
P R I M E A U A R E B I
A G S R H E E K C J A B
```

# FLYER'D UP!

Trivia, Facts, and Anecdotes for Fans of the Orange and Black.

# BIBLIOGRAPHY

The Philadelphia Flyers Media Guide

Full Spectrum The Complete History of the Philadelphia Flyers Hockey Club by Jay Greenberg

The Greatest Players and Moments of the Philadelphia Flyers by Stan Fischler

WWW.FLYERSHISTORY.NET

WIKIPEDIA

http://en.wikipedia.org/wiki/History_of_the_Philadelphia_Flyers

WWW.NHL.COM

WWW.PHILADELPHIAFLYERS.COM

WWW.HOCKEYBUZZ.COM

Bill Meltzer's Heroes of the Past

# Chris Tucci

Sports illustration and graphics

Winner of the Philadelphia Sports Hall of Fame
2006 Art Competition

**http://www.biskitart.com**
**http://www.sportsartwork.net**

609-471-0062

**Biskit Art.com**
where art and hockey collide...

# FLYER'D UP!

Trivia, Facts, and Anecdotes for Fans of the Orange and Black.

## AUTOGRAPHS

# FLYER'D UP!

Trivia, Facts, and Anecdotes for Fans of the Orange and Black.

**AUTOGRAPHS**

# FLYER'D UP!

Trivia, Facts, and Anecdotes for Fans of the Orange and Black.

## AUTOGRAPHS

# FLYER'D UP!

Trivia, Facts, and Anecdotes for Fans of the Orange and Black.

**AUTOGRAPHS**

# FLYER'D UP!

Trivia, Facts, and Anecdotes for Fans of the Orange and Black.

## AUTOGRAPHS

**AUTOGRAPHS**

# FLYER'D UP!

Trivia, Facts, and Anecdotes for Fans of the Orange and Black.

## AUTOGRAPHS

# FLYER'D UP!

Trivia, Facts, and Anecdotes for Fans of the Orange and Black.

**AUTOGRAPHS**